ACCESS 2002

in easy steps

STEPHEN COPESTAKE

KU-943-849

BIRKBECK LIBRARY COLLEGE

In easy steps is an imprint of Computer Step
Southfield Road . Southam
Warwickshire CV47 0FB . England

http://www.ineasysteps.com

Copyright © 2002–2003 by Computer Step. All rights reserved. No part of this book may be reproduced or transmitted in any form or by any means, electronic or mechanical, including photocopying, recording, or by any information storage or retrieval system, without prior written permission from the publisher.

Notice of Liability

Every effort has been made to ensure that this book contains accurate and current information. However, Computer Step and the author shall not be liable for any loss or damage suffered by readers as a result of any information contained herein.

Trademarks

Microsoft® and Windows® are registered trademarks of Microsoft Corporation. All other trademarks are acknowledged as belonging to their respective companies.

Printed and bound in the United Kingdom

ISBN 1-84078-143-2

Contents

Creating forms   **73**

4

Entering/editing data   **99**

5

Using speech recognition   117

6

Querying databases   121

7

Creating reports   133

8

First steps

This chapter shows you how to get started quickly in Access 2002. You'll learn about its screen, work with toolbars then use Ask-a-Question to find specific help. Finally, you'll enhance your use of Access with additional features (these include automatic menu/toolbar customisation; Quick File Switching; repairing program and file errors; copying/pasting multiple data items; using the Task Pane; and saving configuration settings) and protect your databases in various ways by making them more secure.

Covers

Chapter One

The Access 2002 screen

Below is a detailed illustration of a typical Access 2002 screen:

This is Datasheet view, one of several ways of viewing and interacting with your data.

(See chapter 4 for more information on views).

In certain situations, Access 2002 toolbars prefer to display on separate rows.

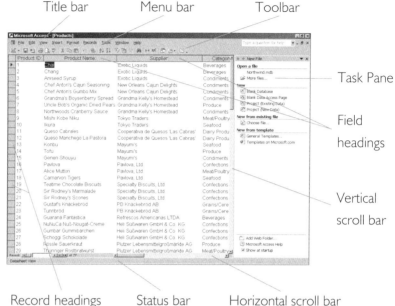

Title bar   Menu bar   Toolbar

Task Pane

Field headings

Vertical scroll bar

Record headings   Status bar   Horizontal scroll bar

You can also hide or show specific toolbars – see the facing page.

Some of these – e.g. the scroll bars – are standard to all programs which run under Windows. One – the Status bar – can be hidden, if required.

Specifying whether the Status bar displays

Pull down the Tools menu and click Options. Then do the following:

If you want to hide the Task Pane, untick Startup Task Pane.

(For more on the Task Pane, see page 18.)

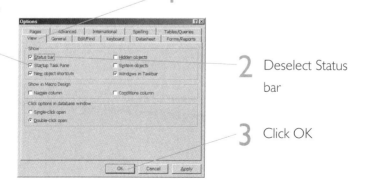

Ensure the View tab is active

2 Deselect Status bar

3 Click OK

Toolbars

To add a new button to a toolbar, right-click over the toolbar. Click Customize. In the dialog which launches, click the Commands tab. In the Categories field, click a category (a group of associated icons). In the Commands box, drag a button onto the toolbar in the open document. Finally, click Close.

Toolbars are important components in Access 2002. A toolbar is an on-screen bar which contains shortcut buttons. These symbolise and allow easy access to often-used commands which would normally have to be invoked via one or more menus.

For example, Access 2002's Form View toolbar lets you:

- save and print

- perform copy-and-paste and cut-and-paste operations

- launch Print Preview

- switch to different views

- launch HELP

by simply clicking the relevant button.

Access 2002 provides numerous toolbars. We'll be looking at many of these in more detail as we encounter them. For the moment, some general advice:

Not all toolbars are available at any one time. For example, by default Datasheet view only provides access to the following toolbars:

- *Form View*

- *Formatting (Datasheet)*

- *Task Pane*

- *Web*

Specifying which toolbars are displayed

Pull down the View menu and click Toolbars. Now do the following:

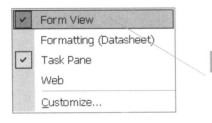

Click the toolbar you want to be visible – a ✔ appears against it

To hide a toolbar which is currently on-screen, click any entry which already has ✔ against it.

Repeat this procedure for as many toolbars as necessary.

Automatic customisation

As you use Access, individual features are dynamically promoted or demoted in the relevant menus.

This means menus are continually evolving...

Until Access 2000, it was true that, although different users use different features, no allowance had been made for this: the same features displayed on everyone's menus and toolbars...

Now, however, menus and toolbars are personalised in Access 2002.

Personalised menus

When you first run Access, its menus display the features which Microsoft believes are used 95% of the time. Features which are infrequently used are not immediately visible. This is made clear in the illustrations below:

Access menus expand automatically. Simply pull down the required menu, (which will at first be abbreviated) then wait a few seconds: it expands to display the full menu.

However, to expand a menu manually, click here on the chevrons at the bottom:

The Edit menu,

as it first

appears...

Automatic customisation also applies to toolbars. Note the following:

• *if possible, they display on a single row*

• *they overlap when there isn't enough room on-screen*

• *icons are 'promoted' and 'demoted' like menu entries*

• *demoted icons are shown in a separate fly-out, reached by clicking:*

...the expanded

menu

Ask-a-Question

In Access 2000, users had to run the Office Assistant (see the tip) to get answers to plain-English questions. In Access 2002, however, this isn't the case. Simply do the following:

Type in your question here and press Enter

The Office Assistant is turned off by default. To turn it on, pull down the Help menu and click Show Office Assistant.

The Assistant is an animated (and frequently unpopular) helper which answers questions, but you can achieve the same effect more easily with Ask-a-Question.

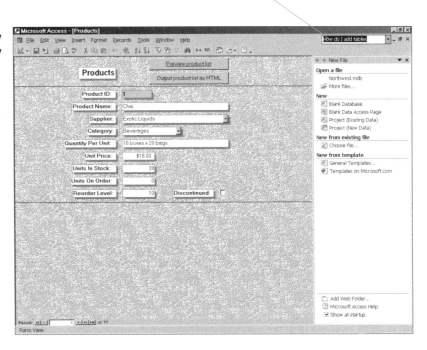

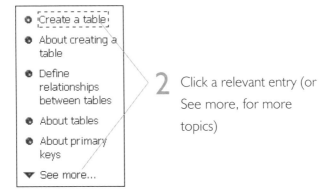

2 Click a relevant entry (or See more, for more topics)

3 Optional – click Show All to display all sub-topics

Use the Contents and Index tabs as you would in any other program.

4 Or click an individual topic

The result of step 3 – all the topics are enlarged (the expanded text is shown in green)

To print out a topic, click this icon:

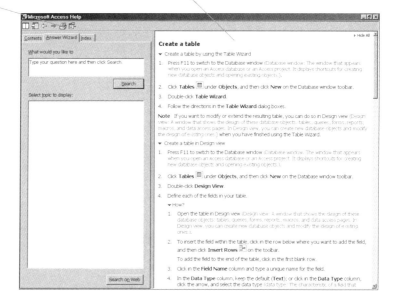

Using Access 2002's HELP system

Access supports the standard Windows HELP system. For instance:

- Moving the mouse pointer over toolbar buttons produces an explanatory HELP bubble:

- You can move the mouse pointer over fields in dialogs, commands or screen areas and produce a specific HELP box. Carry out the following procedure to achieve this:

Access 2002 calls these highly specific HELP bubbles 'ScreenTips'.

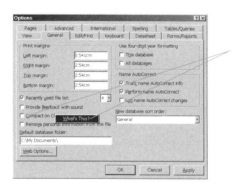

Right-clicking a field and left-clicking the box which appears...

Select to automatically compact and repair your database or compact your Microsoft Access project when you close the database.

...produces a specific HELP topic

Other standard Windows HELP features are also present; see your Windows documentation for how to use these.

Collect and Paste

You can copy multiple items to the Office Clipboard from within any Windows program which supports copy-and-paste, but you can only paste in the last one (except in Office modules).

If you want to copy-and-paste multiple items of data into a document, you can now copy as many as 24 items. These are stored in a special version of the Windows Clipboard called the Office Clipboard, which in turn is accessed by means of the Task Pane. The Office Clipboard displays a visual representation of the data.

Using the Office Clipboard

Use standard procedures to copy multiple examples of data – after the first copy, the Clipboard appears in the Task Pane. Do the following, in the same or another module:

To clear the contents of the Office XP Clipboard, click Clear All.

To call up the Office Clipboard at any time, pull down the Edit menu and click Office Clipboard.

Click the data you want to insert – it appears at the insertion point

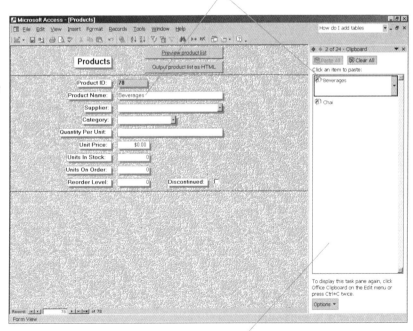

Copying items bigger than 4 Mb (with up to 64 Mb of RAM) or 8 Mb (with more than 64 Mb) to the Office Clipboard will mean it can accept no further data.

The Clipboard Task Pane – see page 18

Quick File Switching

In order to use Quick File Switching you need to be using:

- *Windows 98/2000/Me/XP, or:*
- *Windows 95 with Internet Explorer 4.0 (or a later version)*

Some features in Access 2002 may not have been installed on your hard disk or server (although the relevant menu entries exist in the usual way). These include:

- *the sample Northwind database supplied with Access*
- *specific import filters (e.g. the filter which lets you import CorelDRAW data)*
- *the report Snapshot viewer*
- *some foreign-language fonts*

Access calls this 'Install on Demand'.

When you invoke a menu entry for a feature which hasn't yet been installed, Access launches a special dialog. Complete this as appropriate, then insert the installation CD when prompted or (in the case of networked users) refer to the relevant server location.

In the past, only programs (not individual windows within programs) displayed on the Windows Taskbar. With Access 2002, however, all open windows display as separate buttons.

In the following example, three database components have been loaded. All three display as separate windows, although only one copy of Access 2002 is running:

Three Access 2002 windows

This is clarified by a glance at the Window menu which (as before) shows all open windows:

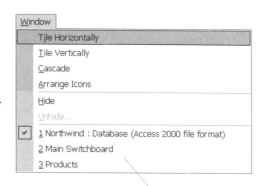

Entries for the three Access windows

Use this technique to go to a document window by simply clicking its Taskbar button, a considerable saving in time and effort.

Repairing errors

Access 2002 provides a special feature you can use to repair damage.

Detect and Repair

Do the following to correct program errors – but note selecting Discard my customized settings and restore default settings in step 2 will ensure that all default Access settings are restored, so any you've customised will be lost. These include:

If Access crashes with a database open, it produces this message:

Ensure Repair my open database... is ticked and click Don't Send. Access restarts, creates a copy of the previously open file and adds _Backup to the end of the first part of the filename. For example, a file called new.mdb will become:

new_Backup.mdb

unless a file of this name already exists (in which case, you're asked to supply another name).

Finally, Access compacts and repairs the original file.

- menu/toolbar positions

- recently used files in the File menu

- view settings

- the size of the Access window

1 Pull down the Help menu and select Detect and Repair

2 Select one or both options

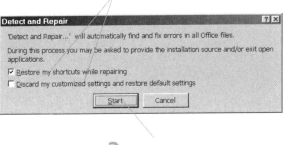

3 Click here

4 Follow the on-screen instructions – Detect and Repair can be a lengthy process

5 You may have to re-enter your user name and initials when you restart Access

Compaction and repair

You can also repair individual Access files. At the same time as it repairs them, Access also compresses them. This is useful because deleting data or objects in databases means that the file can become fragmented and doesn't make the best use of hard disk space.

Compact and repair your databases frequently.

Compaction makes a copy of the relevant file.

Compacting and repairing the active database

> Pull down the Tools menu and click Database Utilities, Compact and Repair Database

When you open a database, Access often detects if it's damaged and gives you the option to repair it there and then.
(See chapter 2 for more on opening databases.)

Compacting and repairing databases which aren't open

1 Ensure no databases are open

2 Pull down the Tools menu and click Database Utilities, Compact and Repair Database

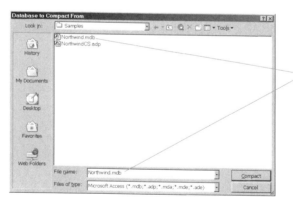

You can have Access compact/repair files automatically when you close them.
Pull down the Tools menu and click Options. Select the General tab and click Compact on Close. Click OK.

3 Specify a database then click Compact (selecting the same name/ address will overwrite the original copy)

4 In the Compact Database Info dialog, specify a destination and name for the compacted file

The Access Task Pane

Access provides a special pane on the right of the screen which you can use to launch various tasks. There are three incarnations of the Task Pane:

The use of the Task Pane is also covered at appropriate locations throughout this book.

- New File

- Clipboard

- Search

Using the Task Pane

To display or hide the Task Pane, pull down the View menu and click Toolbars, Task Pane.

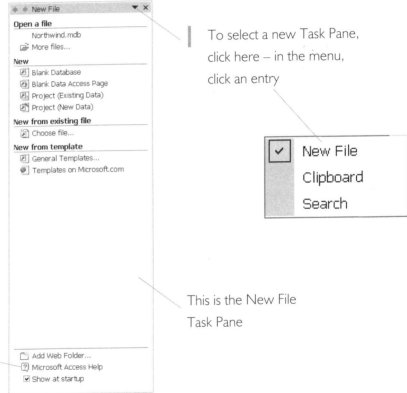

To select a new Task Pane, click here – in the menu, click an entry

This is the New File Task Pane

In the New File Task Pane, click here: to launch HELP.

Saving configuration settings

You could save configuration details on your website, as a handy backup.

You can use a special wizard – the Save My Settings Wizard – to save configuration details in a special file (with the extension .ops). You can then restore the details in the file as a way of transferring your Office XP settings to another machine, or as a backup for your existing PC.

Using the Save My Settings Wizard

1   Close Access (and all other Office programs)

Not closing all modules can result in faulty configuration details being written.

2   Click Start, Programs, Microsoft Office Tools, Save My Settings Wizard

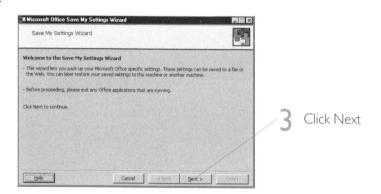

3   Click Next

4   Click Save... to save configuration details, or Restore... to implement previously saved settings

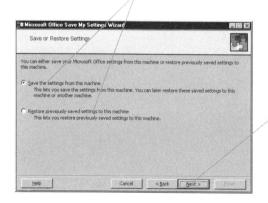

5   Click Next and complete the subsequent dialogs

Database security

You can use a variety of measures to make your databases more secure.

The three security features described here are in (roughly) ascending order of effectiveness.

Encryption

When you encrypt a database, you produce a copy which is compacted AND unintelligible to other software.

> If you have full access rights to a database, pull down the Tools menu and click Security, Encrypt/Decrypt Database

There is a further security feature you can use: user-level security. While password-protection is suitable for databases which are used by just a few people, user-level security is aimed at multi-user environments. It works via a series of passwords/permissions and limits access to individual components according to who the current user is.

For how to use user-level security, consult your system administrator.

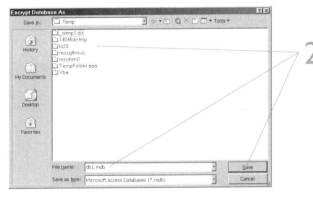

2 Name the encrypted copy, specify an address and confirm

Object hiding

You can conceal objects in the Database window.

> Click an Object type, then an object

See chapter 3 for more on the Database window.

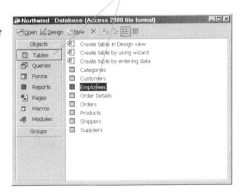

2 Press Alt+Enter

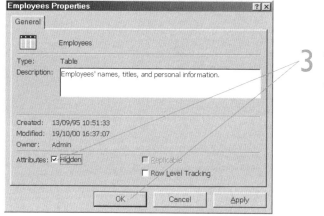

You can also exert some influence on database security via the Startup window.

Pull down the Tools menu and click Startup. In the Startup dialog, untick Database window to stop the Database window from appearing at all when you open the database.

(You can also use the Startup dialog to specify which form automatically loads at startup: click in the Display Form/Page box and make a choice.)

3 Tick Hidden and confirm

Using passwords

You can password-protect a database. This means that anyone wishing to open it is presented with a special dialog:

Enter the password and confirm to open the file

Setting passwords

For more detail on how to open databases, see chapter 2.

1 Press Ctrl+O

2 Use the Open dialog to locate and select the database you want to password-protect

3 Click to the right of Open and select Open Exclusive

Of the three security features described in detail here, password-protection is the most effective. However, it merely restricts access to a database – once it's open, however, users can amend anything they choose.

(User-level security offers greater protection – see the HOT TIP on page 20.)

When you access databases on the web with Internet Explorer 4.0 or later, you can make use of an additional security feature. Access 2002 will only open or download databases which are allocated the following 'zones':

- *Local intranet*
- *Trusted sites*

To allocate a zone to a specific site, choose Tools, Options in Internet Explorer. In the Internet Options dialog, select the Security tab. Click the Local intranet or Trusted sites icon (as appropriate) then the Sites button. Complete the dialog which launches e.g. if you clicked Trusted sites, type in the web address of the 'safe' site you want to access. Confirm the operation.

4 Choose Tools, Security, Set Database Password

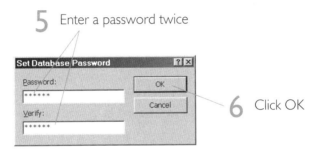

5 Enter a password twice

6 Click OK

Removing passwords

1 Open the password-protected database

2 Enter the relevant password and click OK

3 Pull down the Tools menu and click Security, Unset Database Password

4 Enter the password

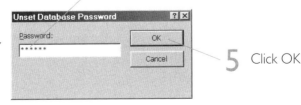

5 Click OK

Your first database

This chapter shows you how to create new databases quickly. You'll learn about database terminology then go on to create a database manually. You'll also automate the creation of more complex examples via wizards. You'll open existing databases, then save your work to disk and export it to Access 2002 and 97 formats. Finally, you'll create shortcuts to web/FTP sites and intranets; learn about the different ways to save data to them (including static/dynamic HTML and XML formats); and publish/merge data directly to Word 2002.

Covers

Chapter Two

Basic database terminology

Before you can learn to use Access 2002 to create databases, you need to be familiar with and understand the following terms:

Database   Information grouped together (and organised for ease of reference) into an Access 2002 file

Tables   Used to store data in rows and columns, like a spreadsheet

Records   (Horizontal) rows of data in tables. Each record is a complete set of related data items. For instance, in a magazine's subscription database each record is (typically) the information associated with each subscriber

Fields   (Vertical) columns of data in tables. Fields are spaces reserved for specified data (for instance, subscription payment details for all records in a magazine database might be kept in a field called 'Renewals')

Fields

First Name	Last Name	Home Address	City
Karl	Jablonski	722 DaVinci Bl	Kirkland
Elizabeth	Lincoln	1900 Oak St.	Vancouver
Nancy	Davolio	507 - 20th Ave.	Seattle
Janet	Leverling	4110 Old Redm	Redmond
Laura	Callahan	4726 - 11th Ave	Seattle
Steven	Buchanan	Coventry House	London
Hari	Kumar	90 Wadhurst R	London
Patricio	Simpson	Cerrito 333	Buenos Aires
Yoshi	Latimer	2732 Baker Blv	Eugene
Lino	Rodriguez	Estrada da saú	Lisboa
Art	Braunschweiger		
Robert	King	7 Houndstooth F	London

Records

Query   The process by which data can be extracted from tables in accordance with criteria you specify. Queries represent ways of viewing fields from more than one table or query in the same record

Forms   You use forms to display table or query data in a customised format. As with queries, forms can host information from one or more tables or queries. Below is a sample form:

Fields

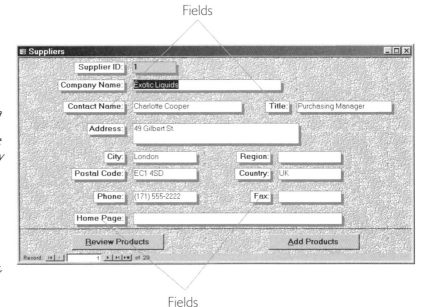

Forms display one record at a time, and are often the most convenient way to interact with your data.

Fields

Tables, queries, forms and reports are all 'objects'. In Access 2002, objects are items which can be selected/manipulated.

Reports   Use reports to display table or query data in a customised format (with page numbers and headings). Reports can't be edited, but they can contain data from one or more tables or queries

The pre-planning stage

Before you start to create a database, it's a good idea to plan it out first. This can save you a lot of time and effort. Consider implementing the following suggestions:

- If you'll be basing your new database on an existing one (manual or computerised), study the ways in which your data is currently organised. This will help when it comes to creating Access 2002 tables and queries

- Make sure you're clear in your own mind about the categories into which data can be split logically. For example, a magazine would clearly wish to have a section where subscription details were maintained, and arguably a separate section for payment details

- Plan out which fields you want your new database to have. For example, a magazine (and most other database types) would need fields relating to:

  - Client names

  - Addresses

  - Phone numbers

A table excerpt from a database storing membership details.
Logically, this field could be the primary key:

- Determine which fields within specific tables can serve as 'primary keys'. The primary key is the field which is common to each record, and which identifies it as being unique. In our magazine example, this could well be the Member ID field. Primary keys are also used by Access 2002 to determine the order in which records are sorted, and to speed up query processing

Member ID	First Name	Last Name	Home Address
1 Karl	Jablonski	722 DaVinci Blv
2 Elizabeth	Lincoln	1900 Oak St.
3 Nancy	Davolio	507 - 20th Ave.
4 Janet	Leverling	4110 Old Redm
5 Laura	Callahan	4726 - 11th Ave
6 Steven	Buchanan	Coventry House
7 Hari	Kumar	90 Wadhurst R
8 Patricio	Simpson	Cerrito 333
9 Yoshi	Latimer	2732 Baker Blv
10 Lino	Rodriguez	Estrada da saúc
11 Art	Braunschweiger	
12 Robert	King	7 Houndstooth F
(AutoNumber)			

Creating databases – an overview

There are two ways to create new databases in Access 2002:

- manually

- using an appropriate wizard

Both approaches have their merits. The manual method provides more precision: you create a blank database and then include the necessary components over a period of time. This method gives you complete control over the make-up of your database, but the process can easily become long-winded. See pages 28–29 for how to do this.

The wizard method, on the other hand, is much easier to use, far more convenient and almost as effective. You can select and apply the Database Wizard you need. When you do so, the wizard automatically inserts the necessary objects in accordance with your specifications.

Database Wizards let you specify:

- the overall form background (you can choose from 10 preset colours and patterns)

- report styles

- which tables and fields should be included

- an overall database title

See the techniques discussed in later chapters for how to customise and supplement manually created databases.

Wizards also let you opt to add pictures to reports.

Although they don't permit quite the same complexity as the manual method, wizards do have the advantage of creating databases which are tailor-made for the purpose for which they were designed. They represent a fast, convenient and detailed method for the creation of databases.

Whichever method you use to create a database, you can easily amend it later.

Creating databases manually

To create a database manually from within Access 2002, pull down the File menu and do the following:

To create a simple database at startup, press Ctrl+Esc. Select New Office Document in the Start menu. In the New Office Document dialog, select the General tab. Double-click Blank Database. Now carry out steps 3–7 on the facing page.

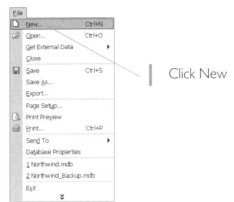

Click New

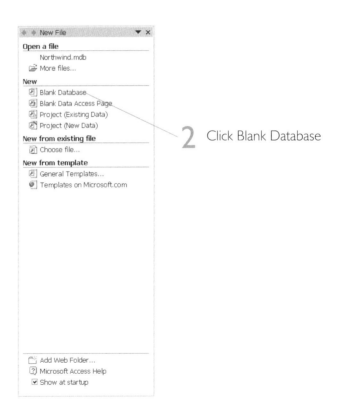

2 Click Blank Database

Repeat step 4 as often as necessary, until you locate the relevant folder.

3 Click here; select the drive you want to host the new database

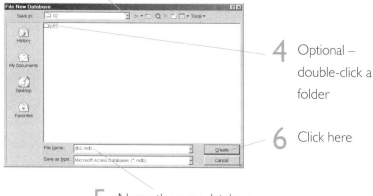

4 Optional – double-click a folder

6 Click here

5 Name the new database

Re step 7 – at this point you can, if you want to, automate the creation of a table with the use of a wizard. See the 'Automating table creation' topics in Chapter 3 for how to do this.

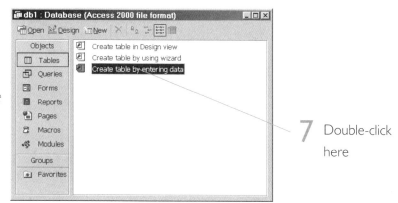

7 Double-click here

After step 7 above, Access 2002 launches a straightforward database in Datasheet view (this is a way of viewing database data which is strongly reminiscent of spreadsheets – see Chapter 5 for more information).

Automating database creation

To create a database with the help of a Database Wizard, pull down the File menu and click New. Now do the following:

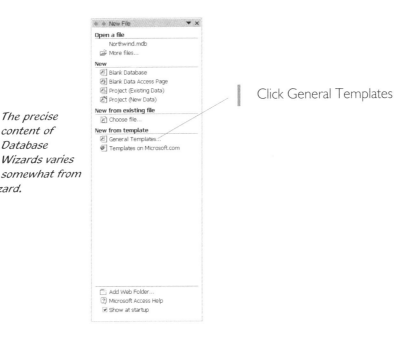

The precise content of Database Wizards varies somewhat from wizard to wizard.

1 Click General Templates

2 Select the Databases tab

3 Select a template and confirm

4 Follow steps 3–6 on page 29

A statement of the new database's functions

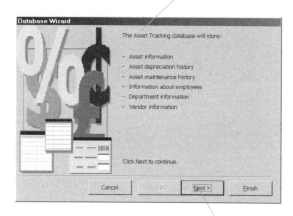

5 Click here

Repeat steps 6 and 7 as often as necessary, then carry out step 8.

6 Select a table for customisation

Re step 7 – to include extra fields, click any italicised entry.

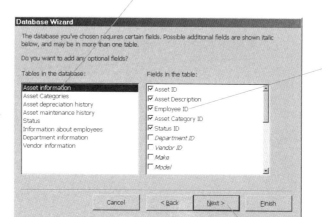

7 Click one or more ticked fields (to exclude them)

8 Click here

...cont'd

Carry out the following additional steps:

9 Select a background

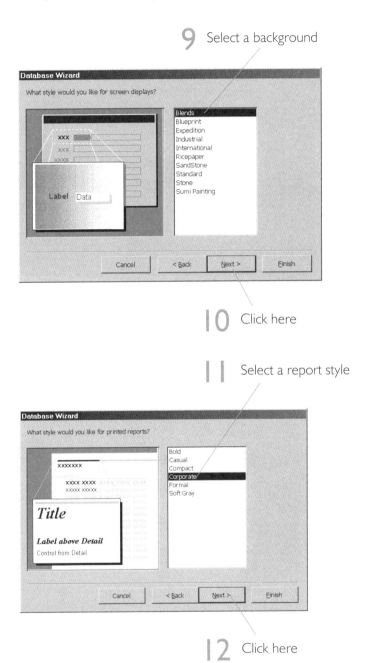

10 Click here

11 Select a report style

12 Click here

32 | Access 2002 in easy steps

Finally, do the following:

| 3 Give the database a title

If you want a picture inserted on reports, click Yes, I'd like to include a picture. Then click the Picture button. Use the Insert Picture dialog to locate the picture, then double-click it.

Finally, carry out steps 14–15.

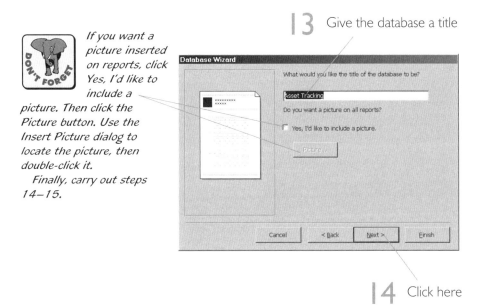

| 4 Click here

Before you perform step 15, ensure 'Yes, start the database' is ticked if you want to have Access 2002 open the new database automatically.

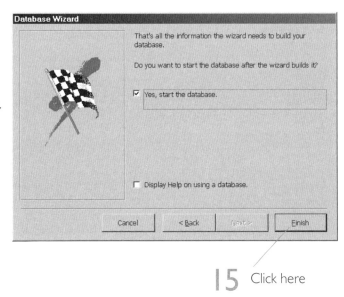

| 5 Click here

Access 2002 now creates the database – the process may take a little while.

Opening existing databases

If the Task Pane isn't visible, choose View, Toolbars, Task Pane.

(If you launch Access 2002 via Start/Programs, the New File Task Pane automatically loads.)

We saw earlier that you can create new databases. You can also open databases you've already created.

Refer to the Task Pane on the right of the screen and perform steps 1–2 (if you haven't recently opened the database you want to open, carry out steps 3–4 instead):

1 If your Task Pane doesn't look like this, click the arrow and select New File in the menu

2 Click an existing database to open it

3 If the workbook you want to open isn't listed, click More files. (Alternatively, press Ctrl+O.)

Re step 4 – if you store workbooks in one folder, you can have the Open dialog default to it.

Pull down the Tools menu and click Options. In the Options dialog, activate the General tab. In the Default database folder: field, type in the default folder. Finally, click OK.

You can copy, rename or delete databases from within the Open dialog.

Right-click any database entry in the main part of the dialog. In the menu, click the desired option. Now carry out the appropriate action.

An example: to rename a database, click Rename in the menu. Type in the new name and press Enter.

4 Use the Open dialog to find and select the database you want to open. Click Open. Alternatively, to restrict the operations that can be performed on the database, click the arrow to the right of the Open button and select Open Read-Only (for a copy you can't change), Open Exclusive (for exclusive access) or Open Exclusive Read-Only (for a combination of both)

Save operations

Most programs require you to save your work at frequent intervals, in order to avoid data loss in the event of a hardware fault or power interruption. However, Access 2002 is different. It automatically saves the record you're working on whenever you:

If you've been working in Design view, Access asks you to confirm the changes before saving. See page 63.

- move the insertion point to a different record
- close the active form, datasheet or data access page
- close the relevant database
- close down Access 2002 itself

You can also save your work manually, if you want (for instance, if you suspect that Windows is about to crash). You can save the active record, or the complete database (including the various layout and design components).

See pages 16-17 for how to correct database errors.

Saving the active record
Pull down the Records menu (if available) and do the following:

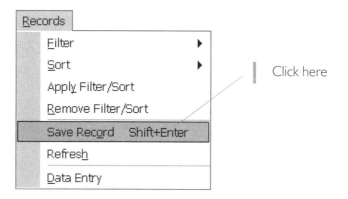

Click here

Saving databases
To save the whole database, pull down the File menu and click Save.

Saving to other Access formats

By default, Access 2002 uses the same database format as Access 2000. This means that you can work with existing databases without the need for prior conversion. Having said this, there is an argument for converting databases to Access 2002 format. For one thing, it has more functionality, works more effectively with large applications and is better set up to deal with any future format changes Microsoft may implement in future.

You can also save databases to Access 97 format, for compatibility reasons. In step 2, select Database Utilities, Convert Database, To Access 97 Format.

Saving a database to Access 2002 format

1 Close all database objects (except the Database window)

2 Pull down the Tools menu and select Database Utilities, Convert Database, To Access 2002 Format

3 Click here. In the drop-down list, click a drive

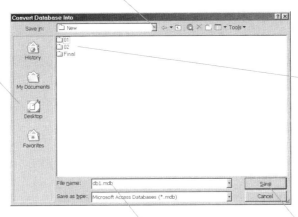

4 Double-click the folder where you want to save the database

Re step 3 – click any buttons here: for access to the relevant folders. (For instance, to save files to your Desktop, click Desktop.) Ignore step 4.

Repeat step 4 as necessary, until you locate the relevant folder.

5 Name the database

6 Click here

Saving to the web – an overview

Preliminaries

See over for detailed information on static and dynamic HTML.

You can save database objects – in a variant of HTML (HyperText Markup Language) or in XML format – to network, web or FTP servers. You can do this so long as you've created a shortcut to the appropriate folder.

With regard to HTML, the above actions are possible because Microsoft has redefined its HTML format.

HTML enhancements

The standard web format (★.html or ★.htm) now incorporates the following:

See chapter 9 for creating data access pages for use on the web.

- it's now a Companion File format (Microsoft regards it as occupying the same status as its proprietary formats); this means that you can create *and* share rich web documents with the same Access 2002 tools used to create printed documents

To import HTML or XML data, pull down the File menu and click Get External Data, Import. In the Import dialog, locate and select the relevant data file. Click OK. Complete the dialog(s).

- it now duplicates the functionality of the proprietary formats (i.e. all the usual Access 2002 features are preserved when saving in HTML format)

- it's now recognised by the Windows Clipboard. This means that data can be copied from Internet Explorer and pasted directly into Access 2002

XML features

You can also publish Access data on the web in Extensible Markup Language (.XML) format, which specialises in describing/ distributing data. Whereas HTML concentrates on describing how web pages look, XML specifies how web data is structured. How it's presented is the subject of a presentation file (called a 'schema') which means that any application reading the XML data can present it in a host of different ways.

If no schema is present, Internet Explorer 5.x displays XML files with an inbuilt tree structure.

Another advantage of XML is that it's platform-independent: it can be utilised across the Internet, by different computers and applications.

Types of web saving

Access 2002 lets you work with several different types of web page. These include:

To use data access pages, your browser must support Dynamic HTML version 4 or above.

Data access pages

Data access pages have a direct connection to database data. You use these to interact with the data via Internet Explorer 5.x or later. You publish your data access pages (plus the database) to a web folder or server to ensure that other people can use them.

See chapter 9 for more on data access pages.

Dynamic HTML

Dynamic HTML files are also known as 'server-generated' files and display as a table in any browser. To create a dynamic HTML file, output any table, query or form to ASP (Active Server Pages) format.

You can also create dynamic HTML files by exporting to HTX (Microsoft IIS 1-2) format – see your system administrator for more information.

Use dynamic HTML:

- for data which changes frequently

- in any browser

Static HTML

You can export any table, query, form or report to static HTML. In browsers, exported reports display as reports while tables, queries and forms display in Datasheet view. There are two reasons for using static HTML:

When an ASP or HTX file is opened or refreshed, what actually happens is that a dynamically-produced HTML file is sent to the user's browser.

- you don't have access to the latest version of browsers (the only stipulation is that the browser used must support HTML 3.2 or later)

- your data is not likely to be updated frequently (if it does change, you have to re-export the static HTML file) and you don't want to interact with it

HTML templates

This is really a sub-class. HTML templates are used to enhance server-generated and static HTML files, and consist of text files with tags which are specific to Access 2002.

Creating shortcuts

To create a
shortcut to a
web/FTP
folder, you
must have:

- a live Internet connection
- rights to view/save files
- its URL

To create a shortcut to an
intranet folder, you must
have the following:

- a network connection
- rights to view/save files
- its network address

To create a web
folder, first get
details of
servers which
support web
folders from your:

- system administrator

or

- Internet Service Provider

Re step 2 –
users of
Windows 2000
or Me should
click My
Network Places instead. In
step 3, double-click Add
Network Place and complete
the Add Network Place
wizard.

In order to save web-format documents (see pages 37–38 for details) to network, web or FTP servers, you need to have created a shortcut to the relevant folder.

Creating shortcuts to web/FTP folders

1   Open the Open (File, Open) or Export... (File, Export) dialog and do the following:

3   Double-click Add Web Folder

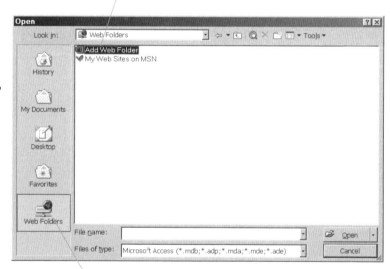

2   In Windows NT 4 or 98, click here

4   Follow the on-screen instructions

Creating shortcuts to local network folders

This requires a different procedure.

Windows 2000/Me users should use My Network Places, while Windows NT 4.0 and 98 users should use Network Neighborhood. (For how to do this, see your system administrator.)

Saving to static HTML

This is the Form View toolbar; other Access 2002 toolbars contain the Database window icon.

If you only want to export a portion of a table, select it before you begin the procedures described here.

You can export database components into other Access databases.

Follow steps 1–4 then, in the dialog, select and double-click the database you want to export to. In the Export dialog, apply a new name to the component (or accept the original). If you're exporting a table, also specify what you want exported:

- *just the data, or;*
- *the data plus its definition (information about the table's design)*

Finally, click OK.

Before you can save files to web folders or FTP sites, you must first have carried out the relevant procedures. See page 39.

Exporting database components

If the Database window isn't currently on-screen, refer to the relevant on-screen toolbar and do the following:

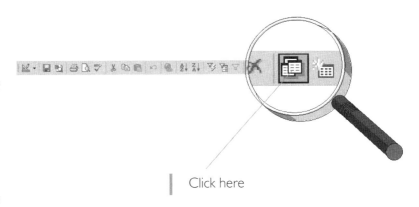

Click here

Now refer to the Database window and do the following:

2 Select an object type e.g. Tables, Queries or Forms

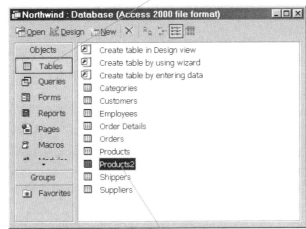

3 Select an individual component, as appropriate

...cont'd

Re step 5 – carry out one of the following procedures according to which version of Windows you're running:

- *Windows NT 4 and 98 users – use Network Neighborhood to save to a local network folder and Web Folders to save to a web or FTP folder*

- *Windows 2000 and Me users – use My Network Places to save to a local network folder or to a web or FTP folder*

Ensure Save formatted is selected to save your HTML file in a format which resembles Datasheet view.

4   Pull down the File menu and click Export.

5   Click here. In the drop-down list, select a recipient – see the DON'T FORGET tip

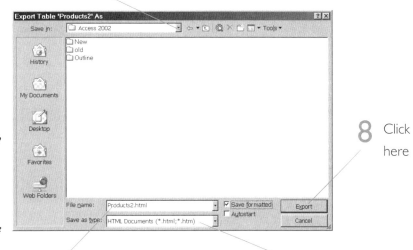

8   Click here

7   Name the file

6   Click here; in the list, select HTML Documents...

9   If 'Save formatted' was selected (see the HOT TIP) Access 2002 launches a special dialog. Do the following to create your HTML file with a default format:

To apply a template to your HTML file, click Select a HTML Template then specify its location.

(Or click Browse and use the resultant dialog to locate and select the HTML template.)

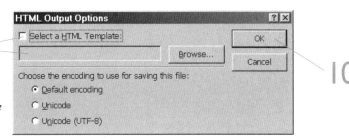

10   Click here

Saving to XML

Export your data to XML if you want to reopen it in Microsoft Excel. (You can also export data to Excel's own format. Simply choose Microsoft Excel... – where the ellipsis denotes the correct version – in step 2.)

1 Follow steps 1–5 on pages 40–41

2 In step 6 on page 41, select XML Documents (.xml)

3 Follow steps 7–8 on page 41

4 Specify what to export

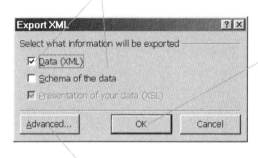

8 Click here

You can 'drag and drop' tables into Excel 2002. With Excel 2002 and Access 2002 on-screen as windows, move the mouse pointer over any table within the Database window. Drag the table into an open Excel spreadsheet.

5 Optional – click here for advanced options (see below)

Advanced XML options

If you carried out step 5, do the following:

Re steps 6–7 – complete the appropriate advanced options. For example:

6 Select a tab

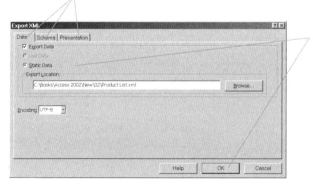

7 Make the relevant changes and confirm

Tab	Action
Data	Specify where the XML file should be saved to
Schema	If you selected Schema of the data in step 4, choose whether to include a primary key and specify an output file name (suffix: .xsd)

Saving/publishing to dynamic HTML

You can't export reports to dynamic HTML.

Re step 2 – you can also select Microsoft IIS 1-2 (*.htx; *.idc). See your system administrator for more information.

The instructions here are guidelines to the overall procedure. Some of the later steps may already have been carried out. Consult your system administrator for more specific information.

Data sources which have had a System DSN allocated can be utilised by any user with privileges.

Finally, if you entered User to Connect As and Password for User passwords in step 4, you can (optionally) define user-level passwords with the same values (see your system administrator for how to do this).

1 Follow steps 1–5 on pages 40–41

2 In step 6 on page 41, select Microsoft Active Server Pages (*.asp)

3 Perform steps 7–8 on page 41

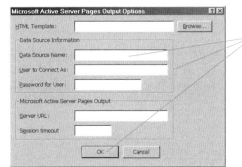

4 Complete these options, as appropriate (in particular, enter a Data Source Name) and confirm

5 On the computer which will process the dynamic HTML files, install the relevant software

6 Create a folder to host the ASP files, then copy the files to it

7 Allocate the relevant privileges

8 Copy the appropriate database to the folder

9 Define the data source as a System DSN (Data Source Name) but make sure you use the name you entered in step 4

Reopening static HTML files

See pages 40–41 and 43 for how to generate HTML files from Access 2002 database components.

Because Microsoft regards HTML as having the same status as its own proprietary formats, when you export HTML files in Access 2002 they can be viewed directly from within Internet Explorer 5.x or later with little or no loss of data or formatting.

The lack of deterioration can be demonstrated further with the help of examples. Study the two illustrations below:

You can edit Access-produced HTML files directly from within Internet Explorer 5.x or higher, but only in Word or Excel. Do the following in the toolbar:

Click here and select Edit with Microsoft Word or Edit with Microsoft Excel

The original database component – here, a table...

Most formatting and features can be brought back into Access. Here, saving the table to HTML and reopening it has produced only one significant change:

- *gridlines are visible (to disable these in Datasheet view, choose Format, Datasheet. In the Gridlines Shown section in the Datasheet Formatting dialog, untick Horizontal and/or Vertical. Click OK.)*

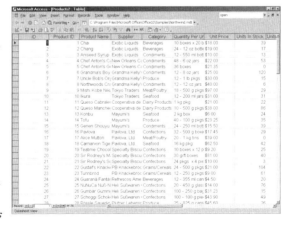

The table's HTML file after being reopened in Access 2002

Publishing data to Word

You can also export data as a text file (delimited, CSV etc.), a RTF (Rich Text Format) file or in any other supported third-party format.

Follow steps 1–5 on pages 40–41. In step 6, select Text Files (*.txt; *.csv; *.tab; *.asc), Rich Text Format (*.rtf) or any other external format. Name the output file and click Export. Finally, complete any further dialog(s) – e.g. in the case of text files, complete the Export Text Wizard.

You can export table, form or report data directly into Microsoft Word.

1 Do the following in the Database window

2 Select Tables, Forms or Reports

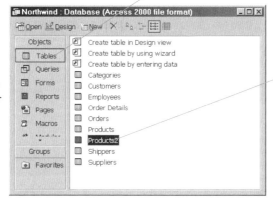

3 Select a table, report or form

If you only want to export a portion of a table, select it before you begin the procedures described here.

4 Pull down the Tools menu and select Office Links, Publish It with Microsoft Word

For how to export data as data access pages, see chapter 9.

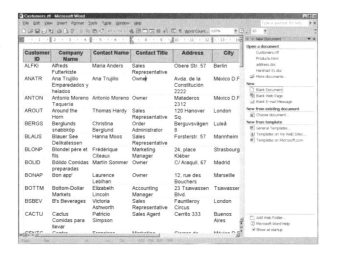

A table after being exported to Word 2002

Merging data with Word

You can carry out mail merges directly from within Access 2002. This exports your data directly into new or existing Word documents.

If, in step 2, you opted to have your data merged with an existing file, complete the Select Microsoft Word Document dialog after step 3.

(In this case, the first incarnation of the Mail Merge Task Pane is different, and there are fewer of them to complete.)

1 Follow steps 1–3 on page 45

2 Select a destination

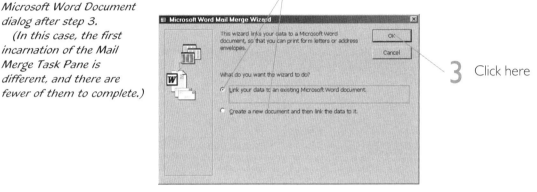

3 Click here

4 Pull down the Tools menu and select Office Links, Merge It with Microsoft Word

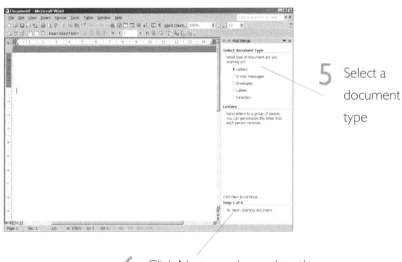

5 Select a document type

6 Click Next... and complete the remaining Task Pane windows

Creating tables

Here, you'll quickly learn how to create new tables and subsidiary tables called subdatasheets. First, you'll learn how to build tables with a wizard. Then you'll discover how to create a simple table manually, and go on to create and edit relationships (data associations). You'll also import tables in Access's own and third-party formats; generate tables from other tables (via queries); plan out/create your own fields and allocate data types; index fields; and customise field properties.

Covers

Chapter Three

Tables – an overview

After you've created an Access 2002 database, the next step is to create the tables which store your data. This is essential if you created the database manually. If, on the other hand, you used a Database wizard to create your database, you'll already have one or more tailor-made tables ready to use – even then, however, you'll probably want to create your own at some time. The procedures outlined in this chapter apply to both scenarios.

All other objects in Access databases (e.g. forms, queries and reports) derive from the data contained in tables.

There are two basic ways to create a table:

- manually

- with the help of the Table Wizard

Both approaches have their merits. On the one hand, the manual method provides more precision: you create a blank table and then (in one or more separate operations) include whatever fields you wish. You can also customise the field formats. This method gives you complete control over the make-up of your table, but the overall process is relatively time-consuming.

The wizard method, on the other hand, is much easier to use and far more convenient. You can:

- choose from a selection of table types

- choose from a selection of table designs

- enter data into the table

- (instead) enter data into a form created by the Wizard

Although using the Table Wizard doesn't permit the same complexity as the manual method, it does represent a fast, convenient, detailed and effective method for the creation of tables.

Whichever method you use to create a table, you can easily amend it later.

The Database window

Preventing the database window from appearing when you open/ create a database isn't recommended, but you can do it if you want – see the HOT TIP on page 21.

To ensure that what the database window is displaying is up to date, press F5.

You can use a keyboard shortcut to display the database window. Press F11.

You can control how items display on the database window:

Click a view icon on the toolbar

To spell-check a database component, select it in the database window. Press F7. (For more on spell-checking, see chapter 5.)

When you create a new database in Access 2002 (or open an existing one), the Database window displays. Since this is the basis for table creation, we need to discuss this before we move on.

The illustration below shows a small, manually created database:

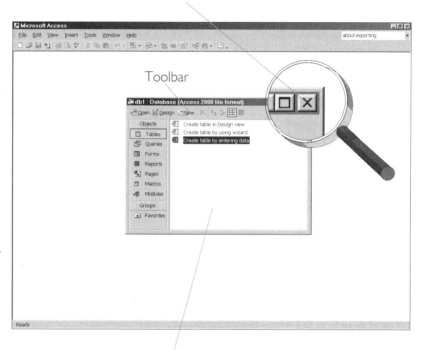

Magnified view of Close button

Toolbar

Database window

The Database window can be thought of as a command centre for the active database. For example, clicking on the Close button closes the database. It's also the basis from which much of the work you carry out with tables, queries, forms and reports is undertaken.

Automating table creation

This is the Form View toolbar; other Access 2002 toolbars contain the Database window icon.

To create a table with the help of the Table Wizard, first make sure that the Database window is visible. If it isn't currently on-screen, do the following:

To monitor additional data in a table, add more fields – see page 65.

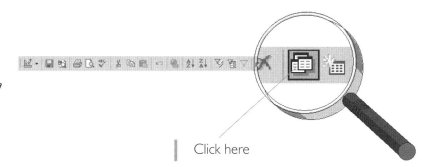

Click here

Data in tables is organised into columns ('fields') and rows ('records'). For more on these (and for a visual representation) see page 24.

Now refer to the Database window and do the following:

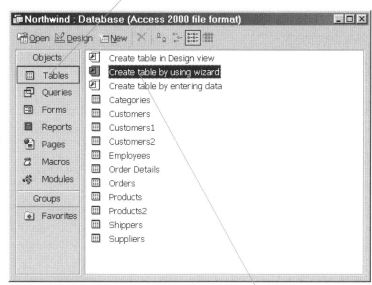

2 Activate the Tables tab

3 Double-click Create table by using wizard

You can also add derivative tables (called 'subdatasheets') to existing tables – see pages 57–58.

The Database window may appear as a minimised bar in the bottom left-hand corner of the screen. Click its Restore button to make it visible.

If you want to rename fields, click the Rename Field button just after you've carried out step 6. Use the Rename field dialog to carry out the operation.

You can also create tables from imported data. With the database window active, choose File, Get External Data, Import. Locate and double-click the Access file whose data you want to import. In the Import Objects dialog, select the Tables tab and double-click a table – Access adds it to the database window.

Re step 9 – it's usually preferable (and quicker) to let Access 2002 select a primary key for you. You can always allocate a new key later, if you want.

4 Choose a table category

6 Double-click the field(s) you want to include – they appear on the right

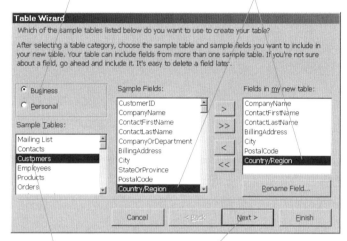

5 Select a sample table

7 Click here

8 Type in a name for your table

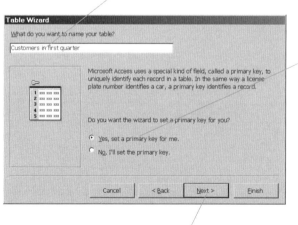

9 Select Yes, set a primary key for me

10 Click here

For more about how to work with relationships, see page 59.

The next stage in the process of table creation has to do with relationships. Often when you build a new table, one or more of the records will be held in common with other tables in the same database. When this is so, you need to tell Access 2002 what the precise relationship is.

Do the following:

If your new table has no common records, simply omit steps 11–13. Instead, merely follow step 14.

| | Click here if your new table is related to another

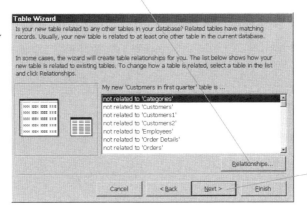

14 Click here

If this is the first table you've created in the current database, neither of the dialogs shown here display. Instead, proceed directly to page 53.

|2 Click the appropriate relationship option

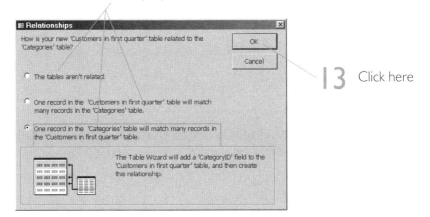

|3 Click here

The Table Wizard is now almost ready to create your table. When it has done so, you'll probably want to begin entering data more or less immediately. Access 2002 lets you do this in two ways:

• directly into the table

• into a form built by the wizard

Each of these techniques has its own particular merits; you can specify which you prefer now.

The table method is more suitable for the rapid entering of information in bulk, while the form method is more visually appealing and – arguably – makes your data easier to work with.

Carry out the following steps:

15 Click a data entry option – see above

Re step 15 – you can also opt to have Access 2002 let you customise the design of your table when the wizard has completed it. To do this, select Modify the table design – Access launches the Design View window after step 16.

For how to use this, see the 'Amending table design' topics (and others) later.

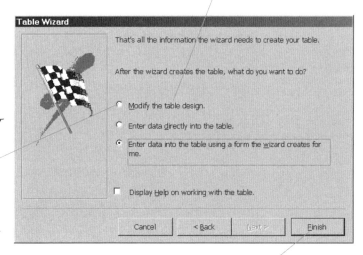

16 Click here

To add new columns (fields) to tables in Datasheet View, click the column to the left of which you want the new column inserted. Pull down the Insert menu and click Column.

(Now apply the relevant data type etc. in Design view – see later in this chapter.)

Access applies a default name (e.g. 'Field1') to new columns. To change this, click the column header. Right-click the column and select Rename Column in the menu. Back in the column header, type in the new name, then press Enter.

The Table Wizard now launches one of the following (according to whether you chose Enter data directly into the table or Enter data directly into the table using a form... in step 15 on page 53):

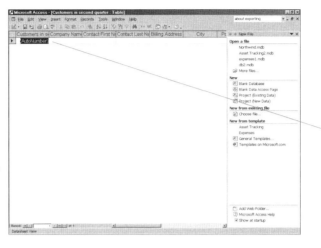

A table containing a single blank record

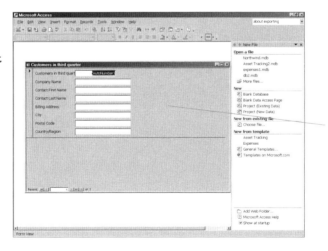

A form showing the first (blank) record in the new table

You can now begin entering data into your new table. (For how to do this, see Chapter 5.)

Creating tables manually

You can generate a table from another table, by means of a query.

In Query Design view, pull down the Query menu and select Make-Table Query. In the Make Table dialog, name the new table and select whether it should be in the existing or another database (if the latter, enter its address). Click OK. Drag the relevant fields from the field list into the design grid and customise them.

(For how to design queries – and for more information on queries generally – see chapter 7.)

To create a table from scratch, first make sure that the Database window is visible. If it isn't currently on-screen, do the following:

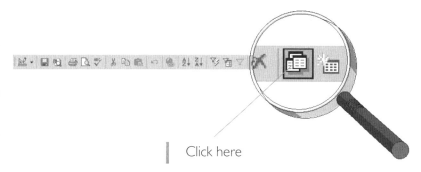

Click here

Now refer to the Database window and do the following:

You can also create a blank table and have Access go directly to Design view. Double-click Create table in Design view in step 3. Then refer to page 65 onwards for how to add the relevant fields.

2 Activate the Tables tab

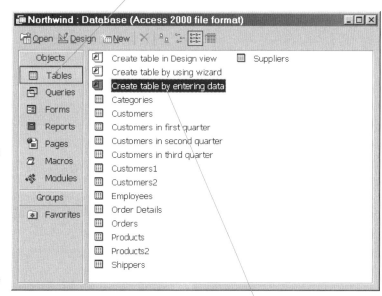

To add a new row (record) to tables in Datasheet View, pull down the Insert menu and click New Record.

3 Double-click Create table by entering data

You can import data in third-party formats into the active database.

When you do this, Access 2002 creates a new table to host the data.

Go to the Database window. Pull down the File menu and click Get External Data, Import. Click the 'Files of type' field in the Import dialog and select a data format. Use the 'Look in' field to select the drive where the file you want to import is located. Go to the relevant folder. Double-click the file.

In the Import Objects dialog, activate a tab and select one or more objects. (Repeat with other tabs, as required.) Finally, click OK.

After step 3 on page 55, Access 2002 creates the new table:

Here, the first field in the first record is highlighted – Access 2002 has automatically positioned the insertion point in it

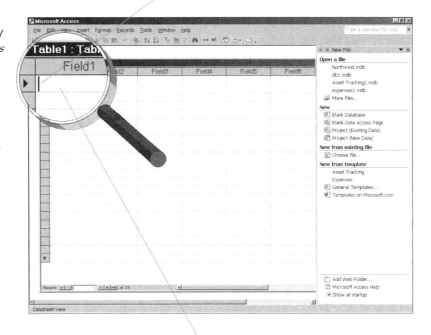

4 Begin entering data straightaway; move to the adjoining fields on the right, as appropriate, by pressing the Tab key

You can (as in step 4) begin entering data immediately. However, it's probably preferable to customise the table's design first.

(Refer to later topics in this chapter for how to do this.)

Subdatasheets – an overview

Use standard 'table' techniques to move around in subdatasheets.

You can add subdatasheets to existing tables (in Datasheet view). Subdatasheets are tables within a table. Tables and subdatasheets complement each other, with the subdatasheet providing further information on the (varying) contents of the main table. Look at the illustration below:

This is the NORTHWIND database supplied with Access 2002; records in the main table display suppliers

If you need to activate a subdatasheet, click the boxed plus symbol. To hide a subdatasheet, click the boxed minus:

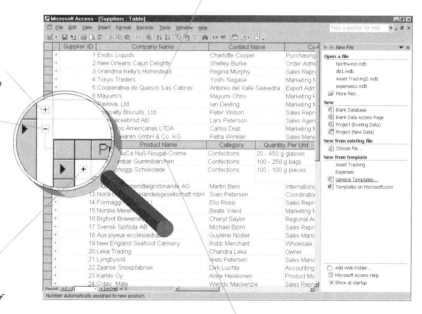

You can insert ('nest') more than one subdatasheet (up to a total of 8) into any given table record.

The flagged subdatasheet shows products which are specific to the supplier selected in the main table

In some circumstances (e.g. in certain one-to-one relationships), Access 2002 automatically creates subdatasheets.

In the above example, each subdatasheet also has a further subdatasheet providing order details relating to each product.

Creating subdatasheets

Open the table into which you want to insert the subdatasheet, then pull down the View menu and ensure Datasheet View is selected. Now pull down the Insert menu and do the following:

 To delete a subdatasheet, open the host table or query in Datasheet view. Pull down the Format menu and click Subdatasheet, Remove.

(Note that no relationships or tables/ queries are affected by the deletion.)

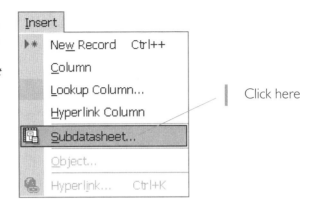

Click here

 Re step 2 – if you want to insert a query (or a table AND a query) as a subdatasheet, select Queries or Both instead. Complete steps 3–6.

2 Activate the Tables tab

3 Select a table for the subdatasheet

6 Click OK

4 Click here; select a matching field from the subdatasheet

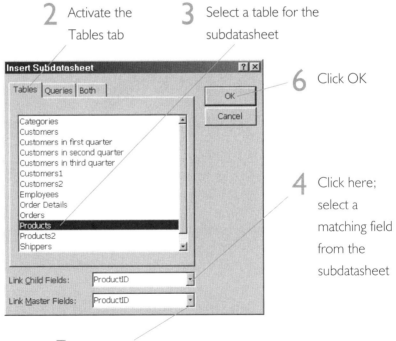

 Re steps 4 and 5 – if you leave the 'Link Child Fields:' and 'Link Master Fields:' boxes blank, Access 2002 inserts all subdatasheet rows into every table row.

5 Click here; select a matching field in the host table

Relationships

If the Show Table dialog isn't on-screen, right-click the Relationships window. Click Show Table.

After you've created tables, you need to tell Access how to associate data. You do this by creating relationships.

Relationships match data in key fields in two tables – usually the fields have the same name. One field is normally a primary key, and the other is called the 'foreign' key.

To view all relationships in a database, press F11. Choose Tools, Relationships, then Relationships, Show All.

The main relationship types are:

*   One-to-many – records in the 1st table match many in the 2nd, but those in the 2nd have only one match

*   One-to-one – records in both tables have only one match

One-to-many is the most frequently used.

To edit a relationship, double-click its join line then complete the Edit Relationships dialog.

Creating relationships

To establish one or more relationships in a table in Datasheet view, pull down the Tools menu and click Relationships

Before you can create or edit relationships, close any open tables.

3 Drag the key field from one table onto the key field in another

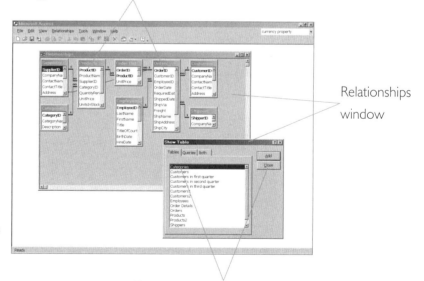

Re step 3 – repeat this operation as often as required. Finally, press Ctrl+F4.

Relationships window

After step 3, the Edit Relationships dialog launches. If you need to, edit the relationship here e.g. to customise the relationship, click Join Type, make the appropriate selection and confirm. Finally, click Create.

2 Double-click the tables you want to relate, then click Close

Table design – an overview

Now that you've created a table manually, you need to customise the field conformation. This involves specifying the following information:

- names

- data types

- format/field size

- additional field properties

To insert the Euro symbol – € – into an Access 2002 field, hold down Alt and press '0128' (minus the quotes) on the numerical keypad to the right of your keyboard. Finally, release Alt.

Available data types

The main data types are:

Text	Use for text and numbers which don't need calculations performed on them (e.g. phone numbers)
Memo	Use for annotations (text and numbers)
Number	Use for calculable numbers
Date/Time	Use for dates (within the year range 100 to 9,999) and times
Currency	Self-explanatory
Hyperlink	The only field property you'll normally need to set for this data type is 'Caption'. For example, if you insert a hyperlinked field containing Internet addresses into a table, you might apply the caption 'Home Page' to it:
	For more information on hyperlinks, see Chapter 5
AutoNumber	Access 2002 uses this to identify records automatically and sequentially

Note that there are three types of AutoNumber. These are:

Increment	Numbers increment sequentially by one – useful as primary keys
Random	Self-explanatory
Replication ID	Used internally by Access 2002

These are set in the New Values and Field Size fields (with AutoNumber set as the data type).

Field properties

The field properties you can set depend on the data type allocated. For example, in fields which have had 'Text' allocated as a data type you can specify (among other features):

- the maximum number of characters data entries can have (called the Field Size)

- the caption (the 'label' for the field when it's used on a form)

- a default value (this is entered into the field as a default in all new records)

- whether the field is indexed (see page 66)

Note that these field properties are common to several data types.

On the other hand, if Date/Time is the data type, you can choose from a variety of date formats e.g.:

- 12 December 2003

or

- 12/12/03

You can also select time formats e.g.:

- 19:32:56 (Access calls this 'Long Time')

or

- 19:32 (Access calls this 'Short Time')

Another example: if you allocate Number as the data type, you can determine:

- the number of decimal places Access 2002 uses to display numbers in the relevant field

- whether scientific notation is used (e.g. $2.16E +03$)

Amending table design

There are two ways to begin customising a table's design.

If the table is already open

Pull down the View menu and do the following:

Changes to the design of a table also affect associated subdatasheets.

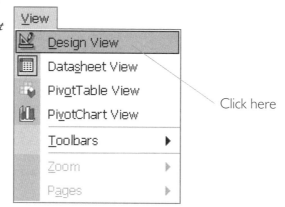

Click here

If the table isn't already open

Make sure that the Database window is visible. If it isn't currently on-screen, do the following:

1 Follow step 1 on page 50

2 Select Tables on the left of the Database window

3 On the right of the Database window, right-click the table you want to amend

4 In the shortcut menu, select Design View

Design View window

The Design View window now launches. There are two sections:

- the Field Format pane

- the Field Properties pane

See the illustration below:

When you close the Design View window, you're prompted to save your work:

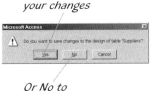

Click Yes to save your changes

Or No to discard them

Field Format pane

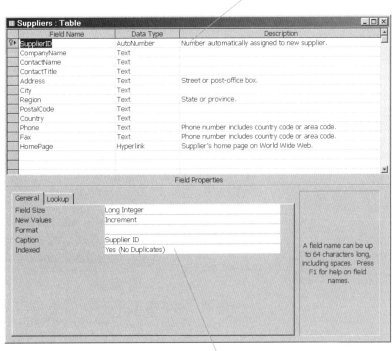

Field Properties pane

You can use the Design View window to:

- set up new fields (see page 65)

- customise existing fields (see pages 66–72)

Planning considerations

Before you start to create fields, it's a good idea to bear the following considerations in mind:

Another source of confusion is the difference between the Currency/ Number and Text/Memo data types – see below.

- what will the field be used to store, and what operations will be performed on the data? For example, a popular area of confusion is the difference between text and numbers. (Access will not store text in a field which has had the 'Number' data type applied to it.)

- will you want to index the field?

- how big do you need the field to be?

- how do you want the data the field will contain sorted?

Currency v. Number

Both of these can be used to store numerical data, but there are differences:

Sorting is an important consideration. For example, you can sort Text and Memo fields, but with the latter only the first 255 characters are used.
  (See chapter 7 for more on sorting.)

Number	Useful for mathematical data (but not for money)
Currency	Values aren't rounded off (up to 15 digits to the left, and 4 to the right of the decimal point), so use for greater accuracy (and money)

Text v. Memo

Both can store text and numbers, but with these provisos:

Text	Use for text and numbers which don't require to be manipulated – can store up to 255 characters (but 50 is the default)
Memo	Can store up to 65,536 characters, so use this if you're feeling expansive

Setting up new fields

Before you can specify field characteristics for a new field you need to name it and apply a data type.

Applying a name and data type to new fields

 Fields which have the following set against them:

Follow the relevant procedure on page 62

Primary Key symbol

are primary keys.

3 Click here

 Changing existing data types (see the HOT TIP on page 66) may take a considerable time if the underlying table is particularly large.

2 Name the new field

 Re step 4 – If you apply AutoNumber (its function is to enter a unique ID reference automatically) as a data type, it usually needs no reformatting (but see the DON'T FORGET tip on page 60).

4 Select a data type

Text
Memo
Number
Date/Time
Currency
AutoNumber
Yes/No
OLE Object
Hyperlink
Lookup Wizard...

Details of Text properties

The next few topics explore the main customisation options which result from specific data types.

You can use the techniques described here to amend existing fields. Areas in which this is often required include:

- *fields which previously contained only manipulable numbers – if you need to add text (and this includes hyphens and brackets), change the data type to Text*

- *the opposite of the above – if you want to perform calculations on numbers stored in a Text field, change its data type to Number or Currency (see page 64)*

Access should convert data accurately when you amend a field's data type. However, Microsoft advises making a backup of the underlying table before you change any data types.

You should index fields you use frequently, and which contain a wide variety of data. An obvious choice for most databases would be the field which contains surname details.

When a field has the Text data type associated with it, you may need to specify:

The character limit

The character maximum for Text fields is 255; often, fields will benefit from having far fewer (one advantage is that Access 2002 processes them more quickly).

A caption

'Captions' in Access 2002 are special titles which only display in forms.

A default value

Default values are text and/or numerals which you want to appear in every instance of the field (e.g. you might wish the 'Country' field in a Contacts database to show 'U.K.' permanently).

Indexing

Implementing indexing in a database often (but not always) enables Access 2002 to find and sort records faster (if it knows where information is, it can usually reach it more rapidly). Indexing only applies to the Text, Number, Currency and Date/Time data types. Fields which have had a primary key allocated are automatically indexed.

When you index a field, you can specify whether duplicated values are allowed; for instance, you may want to allow duplicate names in a Surname field.

Setting Text properties

Launch the Design View window (see page 62 for how to do this). Then carry out any of steps 1–4 below. If you carry out step 4, also follow step 5:

1 Type in a character limit

2 Type in a caption

The arrow indicates that a field has been selected and is being redesigned.

Consider allocating the Memo data type instead of Text – see the lower table on page 64.

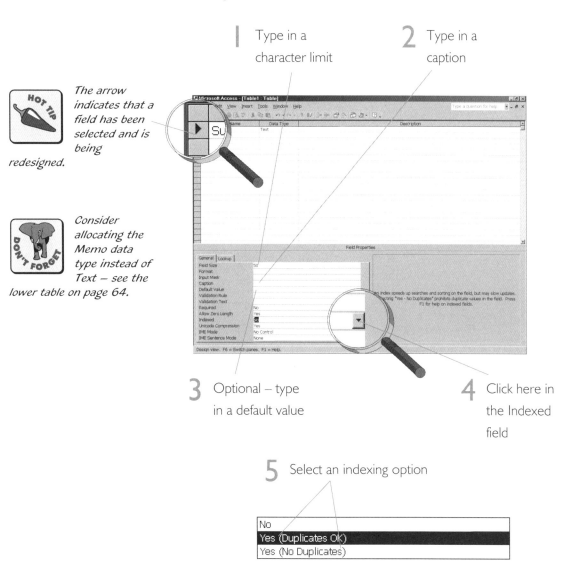

3 Optional – type in a default value

4 Click here in the Indexed field

5 Select an indexing option

| No |
| Yes (Duplicates Ok) |
| Yes (No Duplicates) |

Details of Number properties

Note that Single also stores the following negative values:

-3.402823E38

to

-1.401298E-45

Note that Double also stores the following negative values:

-1.79769313486231 E308

to

-4.94065645841247 E-324

Separators fall into various categories. The main ones are:

List separators	Items in a list are separated by commas e.g.: 12,153,233
Thousand separators	Series of three digits are separated by commas e.g.: 128,456
Decimal separators	A dot separates whole components of numbers from their fractions e.g.: 982.56

If you set a field's data type to Number, features you can specify include:

Field Size

You can choose from a variety of settings. The main ones are:

- Integer – stores whole numbers in the range -32,768 to +32,767

- Long Integer – stores whole numbers in the range: 2,147,483,648 to +2,147,483,647

- Single – stores positive numbers in the range: 1.401298E-45 to +3.402823E38

- Double – stores positive numbers in the range: 1.79769313486231E308 to 4.94065645841247E-324

Format

You can specify the number format for a field's contents. The main choices are:

- General Number – numbers display as entered

- Currency – negative numbers are surrounded with brackets, and Access 2002 uses the thousand separator (see the DON'T FORGET tip)

- Fixed – at least one digit displays, and numbers display with two decimal places

- Standard – as Fixed, but Access denotes thousands with a comma

- Percent – Access multiplies inserted values by 100 and adds '%'

Decimal Places

You can specify how many digits should display to the right of the decimal point – the acceptable range is 0 to 15.

You can also insert Auto. This ensures that the limit specified in the Format setting (see above) applies. If this is blank or set to General Number, Decimal Places has no effect.

Setting Number properties

Launch the Design View window (see page 62 for how to do this). Then carry out steps 1–2 to adjust the field size, steps 3–4 to amend the format and/or steps 5–6 to specify the decimal places:

Note that Decimal Places only stipulates how many decimal places display; it has no effect on how many are stored.

Click in the Field Size field, then click the arrow

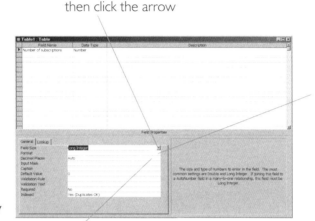

Click in the Format field, then click the arrow

Re steps 3–4 – options you can choose from include the following:

- *General Number – the default*

- *Currency, Fixed, Standard and Percent – these follow the relevant settings in the Windows Regional Settings dialog (see page 70)*

- *Euro – the same as Currency, but uses the Euro symbol*

Click in the Decimal Places field, then click the arrow

Click a field size

The number of digits to the left of the decimal point is specified by the Format setting.

General Number	3456.789
Currency	£3,456.79
Euro	€3,456.79
Fixed	3456.79
Standard	3,456.79
Percent	123.00%
Scientific	3.46E+03

Select a decimal place setting

Re step 6 – select Auto if you want the choice you made in step 2 to determine the number of decimal places.

Click a number format

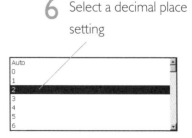

Details of Date/Time properties

To view the Regional Settings dialog, launch the Windows Control Panel. Activate this icon:

If you set a field's data type to Date/Time, there are fewer available features (and many of them have already been discussed in earlier topics). However, you do need to be familiar with the following:

Format

You can specify the date and/or time formats for a field's contents. The choices are:

- General Date – the default. A blend of the Short Date/Long Time settings (e.g. 05/06/03 09:00:12 PM)

  If the data in the field is a date only, no time is shown. And vice versa

- Short Date – same as the Short Date style of the Windows Regional Settings dialog (e.g. 6/12/04)

  Note, however, that the Short Date format shows dates between 1/1/2000 and 31/12/2029 with only 2 digits for the year. For instance, 18th April 2016 displays as: 18/4/16.

- Medium Date – an alternative (e.g. 1-Apr-04)

- Long Date – same as the Long Date style of the Windows Regional Settings dialog (e.g. Tuesday, July 13, 2006)

- Short Time – shows times as an irreducible minimum (e.g. 13.45)

- Medium Time – displays slightly more information than the Short Time option, and doesn't use the 24-hour clock (e.g. 8:32 PM)

- Long Time – same as the settings in the Time tab of the Windows Regional Settings dialog (e.g. 11:52:36 PM)

Setting Date/Time properties

Launch the Design View window (see page 62 for how to do this). Then carry out steps 1 and 2 below:

1 Click the arrow to the right of the Format field

You can create your own customised date/time formats by clicking in the Format field and typing in specific symbols. For example, entering:

dd/mm/yy

would make Access display dates with the day of the month (to 2 digits), the month of the year (to 2 digits) and the last two digits of the year.

(For a detailed list of recognised symbols, press F1 from within Format. Then click the Date/Time Data Type hyperlink.)

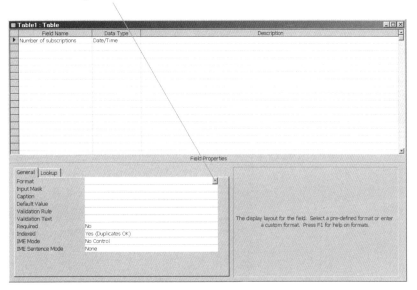

2 Click a Date/ Time format

General Date	19/06/94 17:34:23
Long Date	19 June 1994
Medium Date	19-Jun-94
Short Date	19/06/94
Long Time	17:34:23
Medium Time	05:34 PM
Short Time	17:34

Setting Currency properties

When you allocate Currency as a field's data type, many of the options are more or less identical with those associated with Number. For instance, you can allocate the same Format and Decimal Place options.

Launch the Design View window (see page 62 for how to do this). Then carry out steps 1–2 to adjust the format and/or steps 3–4 to amend the decimal places:

Click in the Format field, then click the arrow

Re steps 1–2 – for details of options you can use, see the DON'T FORGET tip on page 69.

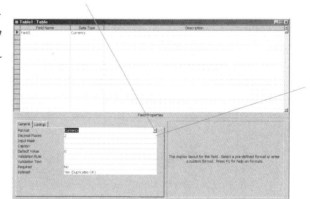

3 Click in the Decimal Places field, then click the arrow

2 Click a number format

General Number	3456.789
Currency	£3,456.79
Euro	€3,456.79
Fixed	3456.79
Standard	3,456.79
Percent	123.00%
Scientific	3.46E+03

Re step 4 – select Auto if you want the choice you made in step 2 to determine the number of decimal places.

4 Select a decimal place setting

Creating forms

In this chapter, you'll create professional-level forms. First you'll automate the process with AutoForm and the Form Wizard. Then you'll create a blank form manually, and go on to create/format dependent subforms. You'll apply preset format schemes; add fields, labels and pictures; import forms from other databases; customise field/label formats individually; create tabbed controls; then apply conditional formatting. Finally you'll analyse your data interactively in PivotTable and PivotChart views and save your work.

Covers

Chapter Four

Forms – an overview

AutoForm is a kind of 'mini-wizard'; it produces simplified forms automatically, based on existing database tables.

Once you've created an Access 2002 database (and possibly one or more tables to go with it), you may well wish to create forms to view your data in a more 'user-friendly' way. If you used a Database Wizard to create your database, you'll already have one or more tailor-made forms ready to use (even then, however, you may well want to create your own at some time). If, on the other hand, you created the database manually, you'll have to create any forms you need. The procedures outlined in this chapter apply to both scenarios.

There are three ways to create a form:

You can import forms from other Access 2002 databases.

From the Database window, pull down the File menu and click Get External Data, Import. Click the 'Files of type:' field in the Import dialog and select Microsoft Access... Use the 'Look in:' field to select the relevant drive. Locate then double-click the Access file which hosts the form you want to import. In the Import Objects dialog, click the Forms tab. Select one or more forms, then click OK.

- using AutoForm

- with the help of the Form Wizard

- manually

All three approaches have their merits. On the one hand, the manual method provides more precision: you create a blank form and then (in a separate operation) include whatever fields you wish. You can also customise the field formats. This method gives you complete control over the make-up of your form, but the overall process is relatively time-consuming.

The wizard/AutoForm methods, on the other hand, are far easier to use. For instance, the Form Wizard lets you:

- choose from six form layouts

- choose from a selection of form styles

- specify which tables/fields are included

AutoForms – see the facing page – display all underlying fields in the associated table or query.

Although AutoForm and the Form Wizard don't permit the same complexity as the manual method, they do represent a fast, convenient, detailed and effective method for the creation of forms.

Whichever method you use to create a form, you can easily amend it later.

Using AutoForm

You can use a slightly different method to gain more control over the AutoForm produced.

Omit steps 1–5. Instead, press F11. Select Forms on the left of the database window and click the New button. In the New Form dialog, select a format-specific AutoForm (e.g. AutoForm: Columnar or AutoForm: Tabular) and the base table or query. Click OK. Access creates an AutoForm using the last AutoFormat you applied (if applicable) or the Standard AutoFormat (see page 90).

To create a form with Access 2002's AutoForm feature, first make sure that the Database window is visible. If it isn't currently on-screen, do the following:

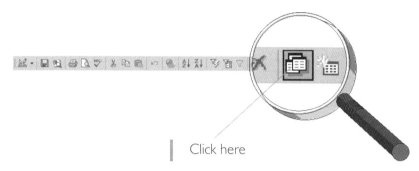

Click here

Now refer to the Database window and do the following:

2 Activate the Tables tab

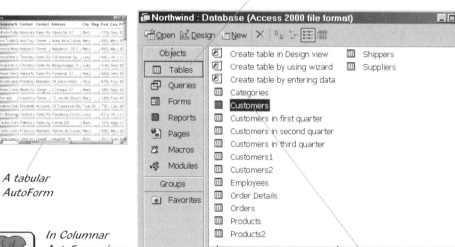

A tabular AutoForm

In Columnar AutoForms (see the above tip), each field displays on its own line. In Tabular AutoForms, each line is a whole record.

3 Double-click a table

Now refer to the Table Datasheet toolbar and do the following:

Other Access 2002 toolbars contain the New Object icon, which looks like this:

4 Click the arrow in the New Object icon

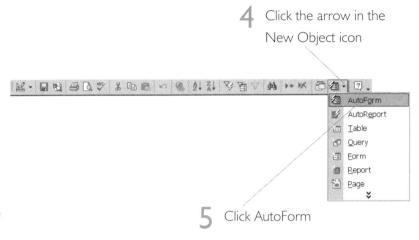

5 Click AutoForm

Use the AutoForm route to form creation when you want to create a form based on a single table or query.

Access 2002 now launches the AutoForm:

In forms created with AutoForm, note the following facts:

• *all fields and records in the base table display*

• *each field appears on a separate line*

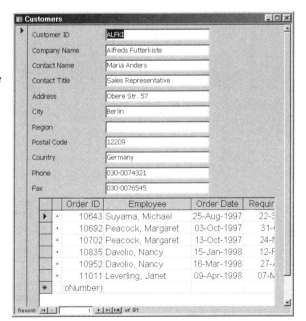

See Chapter 5 for how to enter data into forms.

Automating form creation

To create a form with the help of the Form Wizard, first make sure that the Database window is visible. (For how to do this, see step 1 on page 75.) Do the following:

2 Click New

Use the wizard route to form creation when you want to create a form based on more than one table or query.

Activate the Forms tab

3 Click Form Wizard

4 Click here

Access 2002 now launches the Form Wizard. Carry out the following steps:

If you want to use fields from additional tables or queries, repeat steps 5–6.

You can create a subform at the same time as you create a form. Follow the procedure in the above tip. If the field relationships are valid, carrying out step 7 after you've selected an additional table or query produces an additional dialog. Complete this – in particular, select Form with subform(s).

Finally, complete steps 8–14 to have Access create two forms.

5 Click here; select a base table or query in the list

6 Double-click the field(s) you want to include

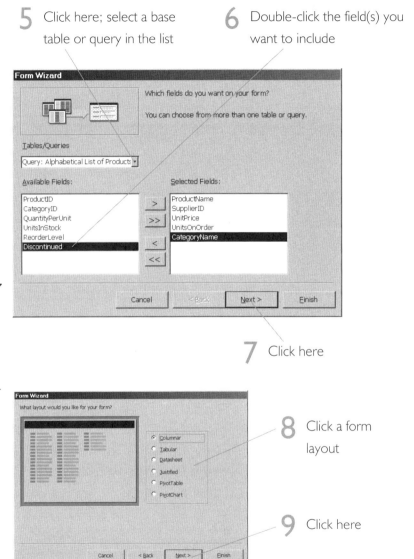

7 Click here

8 Click a form layout

9 Click here

In the final stage in the process of automatic form creation, you select the overall style you want your new form to have. This is especially important in the case of forms because they're highly visual. Do the following:

10 Select a style

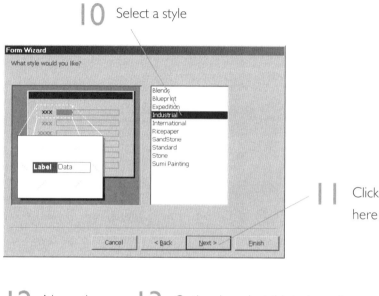

11 Click here

12 Name the new form   13 Optional – select this to have Access open the new form after step 14

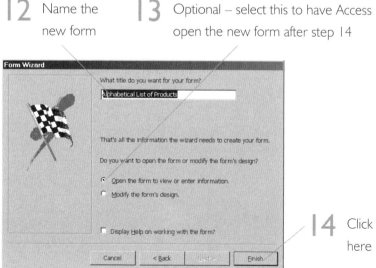

14 Click here

The Form Wizard now creates your new form. It then opens it for editing (if you followed step 13 on page 79).

The illustrations below show two varieties of form (according to whether you selected Columnar or Tabular as the basic layout in step 8 on page 78):

To open an existing form, launch the Database Window (see step 1 on page 75 for how to do this). Activate the Forms tab, then double-click the relevant form.

For details of other form layouts, see pages 84–86.

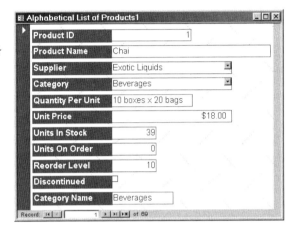

A Columnar form

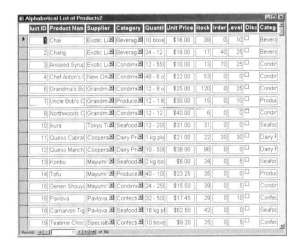

A Tabular form

Whichever form layout you selected, you can now begin entering data into your new form.

For how to do this, see Chapter 5.

Creating forms manually

To create a form from scratch, first make sure that the Database window is visible. (For how to do this, see step 1 on page 75.) Do the following:

2 Click New

Activate the Forms tab

3 Click Design View

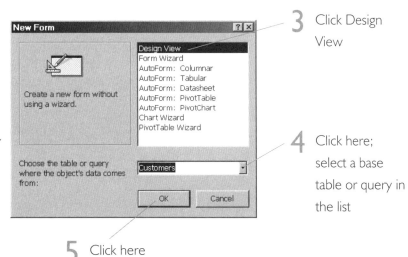

4 Click here; select a base table or query in the list

After step 5, Access 2002 creates the new form in Design view (with easy access to fields in the table or query selected in step 4).

See the 'Amending form design' topics (and others) later for how to customise the new form.

5 Click here

Subforms – an overview

You can add subforms to existing forms. Subforms are forms within a form. Forms and subforms complement each other, with the subform providing further information on the (varying) contents of the form. Look at the illustration below:

As you press: Ctrl+Page Down to view later records in the main form, the subform also changes to display associated data.

This is the NORTHWIND database supplied with Access 2002. Records in the main form display stock categories (the category on display is 'Confections')

This form has had a new AutoFormat applied – see page 90.

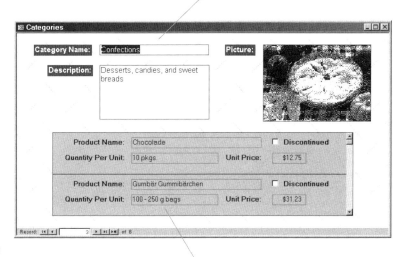

Subforms act like forms. For example, to view subsequent records, first click in the subform. Then press Ctrl+Page Down as often as required.

The flagged subform shows products which are specific to the category selected in the main form – in this case, examples of confectionery and related data

You can insert as many subforms as you want into forms.

You can also insert subforms into other subforms, up to a maximum of 7 – Access calls this 'nesting'.

Subforms can display as:

* datasheets

* single or continuous forms (as above)

Creating subforms

Subforms work best with one-to-many relationships.

Before you carry out step 1, ensure this Toolbox button is selected:

To reformat a subform, open the host form in Design view. Right-click the subform control and select Subform in New Window. This opens the subform in its own design view. Make the relevant changes then press Ctrl+F4. View the host form in Form view to display your amendments.

Re step 3 – you can also base the subform on a table or query. To do this, select Use existing Tables and Queries, instead. Then follow step 4.

After step 4, further wizard dialogs launch. Complete these as appropriate. In the final dialog, click Finish to create the subform.

Open the form into which you want to insert the subform, then pull down the View menu and click Design View. Now do the following:

1 Click this button in the toolbox

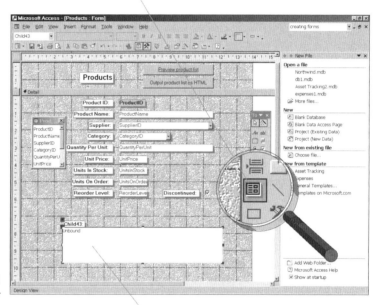

2 Click in the form and drag out the subform area

Access 2002 now launches the SubForm Wizard. Do the following:

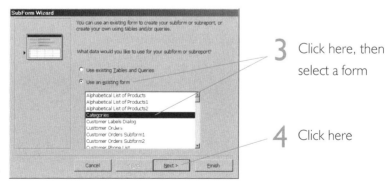

3 Click here, then select a form

4 Click here

Viewing forms

You can view forms in a variety of ways:

Tables are only subject to four views i.e. Form view is not an option.

Datasheet view in a table also resembles a spreadsheet.

- Design view – used to create and redesign/reformat forms (see later)

- Form view – used to view one record at a time

- Datasheet view – used to view forms like a spreadsheet, so you can see multiple records at once

- PivotTable view – you can use this to change form layout on-the-fly. Changes you make are instantly reflected in the form. You can rearrange row/column headings and apply any required filters

- PivotChart view – this is similar to PivotTable view. The main difference is that the data is displayed more visually. You can apply new chart types and dynamically rearrange the series, category and data series fields

You can create forms directly in PivotTable or PivotChart view.

Press F11. Select Forms on the left of the database window, then click New in the Toolbar. In the New Form dialog, double-click AutoForm: PivotTable or AutoForm: PivotChart.

(The above technique is an AutoForm approach. To create a PivotTable with more control over the whole process, double-click PivotTable Wizard instead in the New Form dialog. Complete successive wizard dialogs.)

Switching between views

Pull down the View menu and do the following:

PivotTable and PivotChart views are analysis ('what-if') tools.

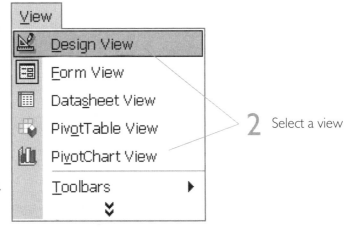

2 Select a view

Using Form and Datasheet views

Use the navigation buttons at the base of most forms to move between records:

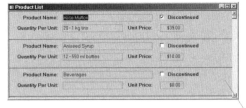

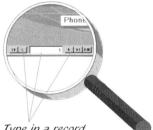

Type in a record no. and press Enter (or click the appropriate arrow)

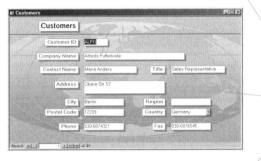

With suitable customisation, forms in Form view can look quite different and more appealing

To add a picture to a form, launch Design view. Click the Image button in the Design toolbox:

On the form, drag out the area in which you want the picture inserted. In the Insert Picture dialog, locate and double-click the relevant image.

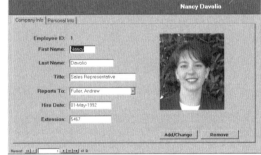

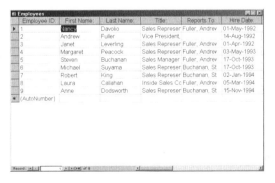

In Datasheet view, however, forms are standardised – use them for bulk data entry

The last two illustrations are alternative views of the 'Employees' form in the sample NORTHWIND database.

Using PivotTable view

To view data in PivotChart view, choose PivotChart in the View menu.

PivotCharts display totals rather than data specifics. Drag any of the fields – and/or apply any filters you need – to update the totals dynamically.

| On the left of the database window, select Tables, Forms or Queries

2 On the right of the database window, double-click a table, form or query

3 Follow steps 1–2 on page 84 (but select PivotTable View in step 2)

4 Drag any of the fields in the Field List window to the appropriate PivotTable area...

This PivotTable is based on the 'Invoices' query in the sample NORTHWIND database supplied with Access.

Fields have been dragged to the various sections of the PivotTable. Also, total fields have been added (to do this, click the Calculated Totals and Fields button in the PivotTable toolbar, select Create Calculated Detail Field and complete the resultant dialog. Then select the field, click the AutoCalc toolbar button and select a function e.g. Count).

The result is that, since PivotTables are dynamic, you can drag any of the fields to new locations (or add new ones) and the data will update. You can also filter the PivotTable by clicking any of the arrows to the right of the fields and deselecting entries. For instance, to exclude USA salespersons (as here), click Country and deselect the relevant entry.

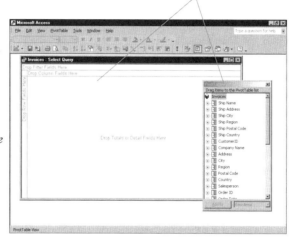

You should drag fields to these areas (clearly marked):

- Filter
- Column
- Row
- Detail

A functioning PivotTable – these are fields

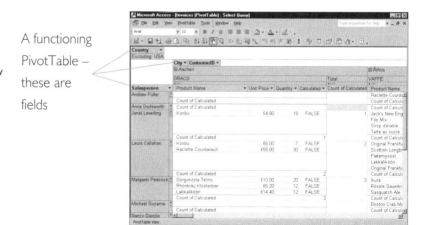

Form design – an overview

If you want to, you can also opt to redesign forms created with the Form Wizard.

After you've created a form manually, you must add the various fields and labels (explanatory classifications) you need. Access 2002 calls everything you add to a form a 'control'. There are two main types:

- bound

- unbound

Bound controls pull in data from fields in an underlying database table. For instance, if a field in a table contains post code information, the relevant control will return post code data for the currently active record.

Unbound controls, on the other hand, contain supplementary text (e.g. instructions to the database user) or graphics components (e.g. lines); they aren't connected to table fields.

The distinction is made clear in the following:

To see what your work looks like, now or at any stage in the form design process, pull down the View menu and click Form View.

(To continue your design work, pull down the same menu and click Design View.)

Bound field

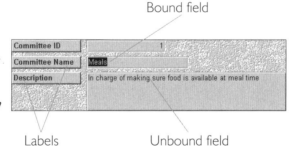

Bound and unbound fields in a form extract

Labels   Unbound field

Bound fields

Bound fields in the original table

Customising form design is much more visual than customising tables.

Amending form design

There are two ways to begin customising a form's design.

If the form is already open

Pull down the View menu and do the following:

When you close the Design View window, you're prompted to save your work:

Click Yes to save your changes

Or No to discard them

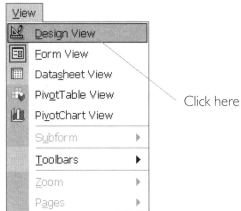

Click here

If the form isn't already open

Go to the Database window (see step 1 on page 75 for how to do this) and do the following:

3 Click Design

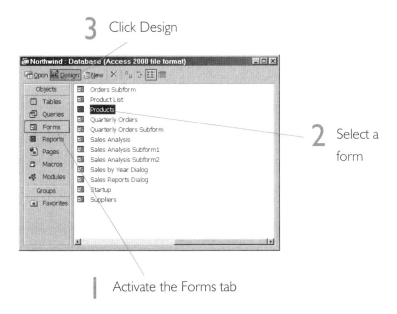

2 Select a form

Activate the Forms tab

If the Field List or Toolbox aren't visible, pull down the View menu and click Field List or Toolbox respectively.

Access 2002 now launches the form in Design View. This is the basis for adding and customising fields. Design View's three principal components are shown below:

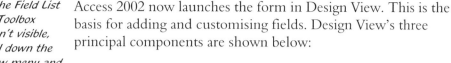

Detail pane   Field List

Here, the Detail pane is uncluttered because this is a manually created form. Detail panes for forms created with the Form Wizard or AutoForm will be more complex.

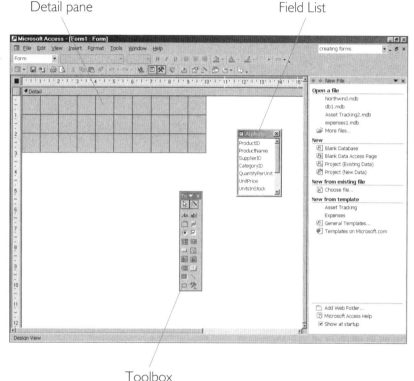

You can add a variety of extra form elements (e.g. tick boxes and option buttons) to forms. Click the relevant button in the Toolbox then drag out the element in the Detail pane.

Toolbox

The Detail pane

You can resize any Design view area. For example, to resize the Detail pane, drag either of its edges (or the corner) outwards. You can also resize or move individual fields.

The Detail pane – see below – represents the current body of your form. Here, you create and design the necessary fields.

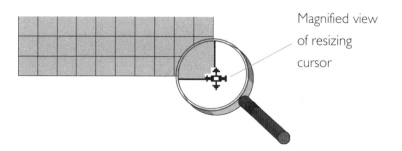

Magnified view of resizing cursor

AutoFormat

You can apply a series of pre-defined formats to overall form design. Use AutoFormat to impose:

- a background

- a preset control font

- a preset control border

Using AutoFormat

With the relevant form open in Design View, do the following to select it:

If the Form Selector doesn't look like this: click it

 If you don't want to apply all 3 aspects of an AutoFormat, carry out step 2. Now click the Options button. Deselect:

- *Font*

- *Color*

- *Border*

(as appropriate) in the extended dialog. Finally, carry out step 3.

Now pull down the Format menu and click AutoFormat. Carry out the following steps:

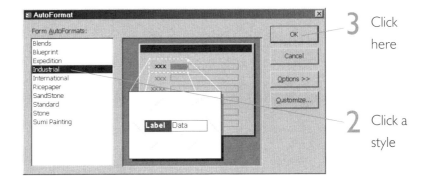

3 Click here

2 Click a style

Conditional formatting

You can have Access 2002 apply conditional formats to fields in forms. Conditional formats are formatting attributes (e.g. a colour or a text style change) which Access imposes on fields when the criteria you set are met. Conditional formats help you tailor your databases to specific situations.

Formatting which alters field size (e.g. font changes) can't be used as a conditional format.

For instance, in a form listing sales results you could specify that sales staff who don't meet a monthly target trigger the display of a specific field providing a warning...

Applying conditional formatting

In a form open in Design View, select one or more fields. Pull down the Format menu and click Conditional Formatting. Carry out step 1 below to set the formatting which applies if the conditions *aren't* met (see the HOT TIP for how to do this). Perform steps 2–3, then step 4 to set the formatting which applies if the conditions are fulfilled (see the HOT TIP for how to do this).

Finally, perform step 5.

Re steps 1 & 4 – click the relevant icon (and, if appropriate, make a selection from the graphical list which appears).

Re step 3 – complete more than one field, if necessary (in line with the comparison phrase chosen).

2 Click here; select a comparison phrase

1 Select the relevant formatting

3 Type in match value(s)

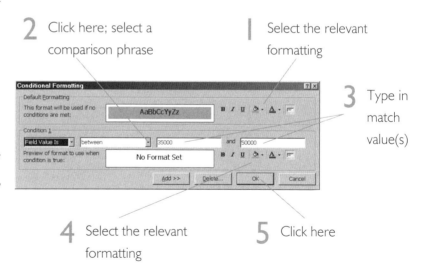

4 Select the relevant formatting

5 Click here

Adding labels

If the form header/footer area isn't currently visible, pull down the View menu and click Form Header/Footer.

It's useful to add descriptive labels to forms. You can add labels to:

- the form header or footer

- the Detail pane

First, refer to the Form toolbox and do the following:

Click here

Re step 1 – if the Toolbox isn't visible, pull down the View menu and click Toolbox.

2 Move the pointer to the appropriate location in the header/footer or Detail pane. Drag to define the label area:

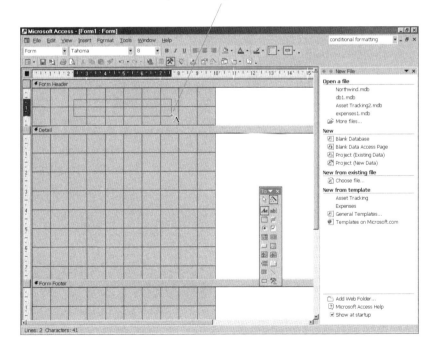

...cont'd

You can add tabbed controls to forms. To do this, click this button:

in the Toolbox. In the form, click where you want the tabbed control to go. This is the result:

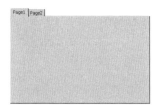

Now use the procedures on pages 92–94 to add the appropriate labels and/or fields.

You'll probably need to reformat most labels after you've created them. (See pages 95–98 for how to do this.)

So far, your label looks something like this:

Label

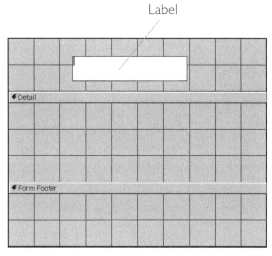

Carry out the next step:

3 Type in the label text. When you've finished, press Enter

The end result:

The inserted label

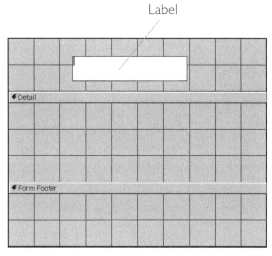

Adding fields

Re step 1 – if no fields appear in the Field list, the probable reason is that you omitted step 4 on page 81 when creating the form: as no underlying table was selected, there are no fields to choose from.

To solve this, right-click the Detail pane. In the menu, select Properties. Click in the field at the top of the dialog which appears and select Form. Activate the Data tab then click in the Record Source field – in the list, select a base table or query. Press Alt+F4 to close the dialog.

Once you've inserted the necessary labels, the next stage is to insert the required fields. This is a simple process involving a drag-and-drop technique.

With the relevant form open in Design View, make sure the Field List is visible. (If it isn't, pull down the View menu and click Field List.) Then do the following:

2 Drag it to the appropriate location in the form

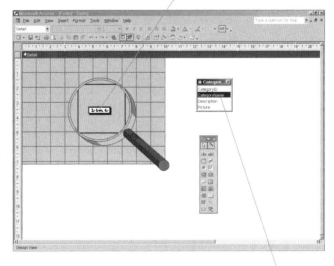

| Click a field

To add new (extra) fields to the Field List, open the table (in Datasheet view) which underlies the form. Follow the procedures in the HOT TIP on page 54 to add a new field. When you reopen the original form, the new field appears in the Field List.

3 The new field is created:

The new field – amend as necessary

Note that fields in Access 2002 forms consist of two parts. These are:

The field name

Title

The field detail

Reformatting labels and fields

If the Formatting (Form/Report) toolbar isn't on-screen, pull down the View menu and click Toolbars, Formatting (Form/Report).

Once you've inserted a new label or field, you can:

• apply a new typeface and/or type size

• align the contents

• apply foreground and/or background colours

• specify a border width and/or colour

• apply special effects

Applying a new typeface

You can select multiple controls by holding down Shift as you click them.

With the relevant form open in Design View, select the control(s) you want to amend. Then refer to the Formatting (Form/Report) toolbar and do the following:

If you want to reformat the field name as well as the field detail, don't forget to select it, too.

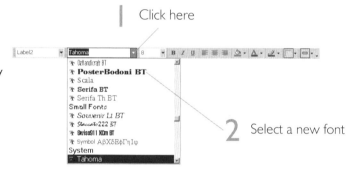

Click here

2 Select a new font

Applying a new type size

If you need greater precision, omit steps 1 and 2. Instead, type in a new type size here: Then press Return.

With the relevant form open in Design View, select the control(s) you want to amend. Then do the following:

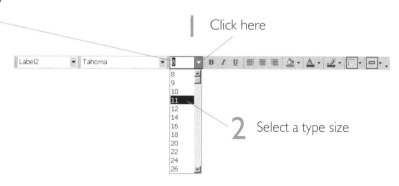

Click here

2 Select a type size

Aligning label and field contents

With the relevant form open in Design View, select the control(s) you want to amend. Then carry out step 1 to left-align the contents, step 2 to centre them or step 3 to right-align them:

For brief details of how alignment works, see the following
examples:

Title	Left
Title	Centre
Title	Right

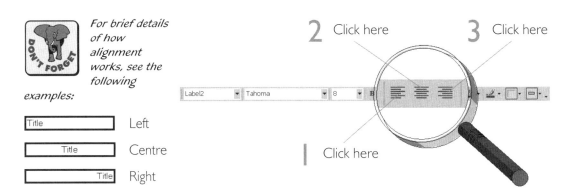

2 Click here

3 Click here

Click here

Colouring foregrounds and backgrounds

With the relevant form open in Design View, select the control(s) you want to amend. Then follow steps 1 AND 2 below to apply a background colour, or 3 AND 4 to apply a foreground colour:

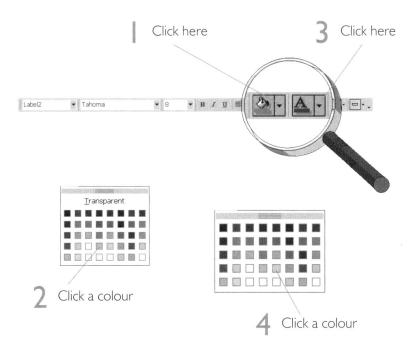

Click here

3 Click here

2 Click a colour

4 Click a colour

Specifying a border width

Access 2002 is supplied with a small number of pre-defined line widths which can be applied to controls. Note, however, that you can only apply the appropriate border to all four sides of a control: you can't specify which edges you border.

First, click the control you want to amend. (If you want to amend more than one, hold down Shift at the same time.) Then do the following:

You must have opened the relevant form in Design View to carry out any

of the procedures here.

To apply a background colour to a control, select it. Then click

the arrow in this button in the toolbar:

In the list, select a colour.

Click the
arrow here

2 Click a border
width

Specifying a border colour

First, click the control you want to amend. (If you want to amend more than one, hold down Shift at the same time.)

Then do the following:

To colour text in a control, select it. Then click the arrow in this button in the toolbar:

In the list, select a colour.

Click the
arrow here

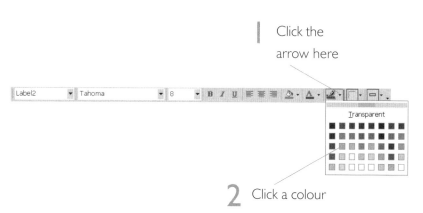

2 Click a colour

Applying special effects

Access 2002 lets you apply several special effects to controls. You can choose from:

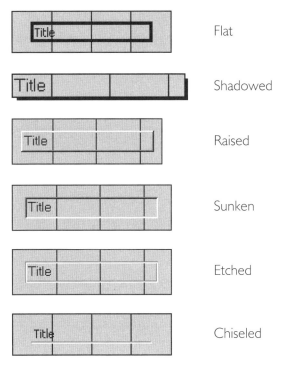

Flat

Shadowed

Raised

Sunken

Etched

Chiseled

You must have opened the relevant form in Design View to carry out the procedures here.

First, click the control you want to amend. (If you want to select more than one, hold down Shift at the same time.) Then do the following:

1 Click the arrow here

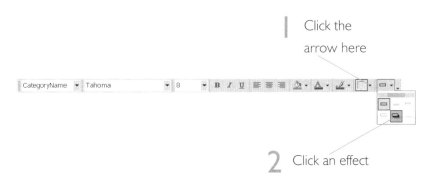

2 Click an effect

Entering/editing data

In this chapter, you'll learn how to insert/delete records, find your way around in complex databases and enter/amend data (including via the Zoom box). Apart from the usual data-entry methods, you'll also handwrite it directly into database components. You'll spell-check data and use AutoCorrect to have wrong spellings corrected automatically. Finally, you'll find/replace specific data; use multiple Undo's/Redo's; sort data alphanumerically; and then insert and use hyperlinks. Finally, you'll learn how to filter databases and save your filters to disk.

Covers

Chapter Five

Inserting a new record

The procedures for entering data are very similar in both tables (datasheets) and forms.

N.B. On this and future pages, the term 'Datasheet view' refers to both tables and forms (when viewed as datasheets).

Before we can go on to discuss techniques for entering data into Access 2002 databases, we need (since this is a necessary prerequisite) to deal with how to create a new record.

You can insert a new record in various ways.

The menu route

In either Datasheet or Form view, pull down the Insert menu and do the following:

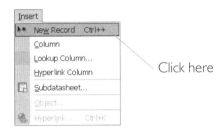

Click here

The toolbar route

If a table is active, refer to the Table Datasheet toolbar instead.

(The New Record icon is unaltered.)

If a form is active, refer to the Form View toolbar. Do the following:

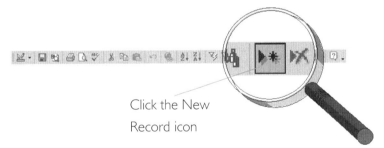

Click the New
Record icon

The Record Gauge route

In Form view or Datasheet view, refer to the Record Gauge in the bottom left-hand corner of the screen. Do the following:

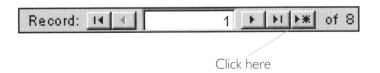

Click here

Entering data

When you've created a new record, Access places the insertion point in the first appropriate field:

To cancel amendments you've made to the active field, press Esc.

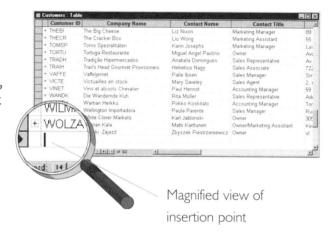

A new record in Datasheet view

Magnified view of insertion point

When you jump to another record (see page 103), Access automatically saves your amendments.

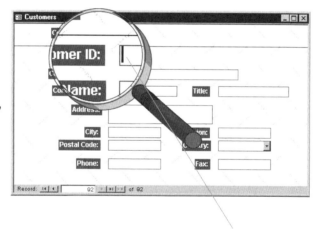

A new record in Form view

Magnified view of insertion point

Instead of pressing Enter, you can also press Tab (Shift+Tab reverses the direction of movement.)

Whichever view you're using, type in the necessary data and press Enter; Access 2002 moves the insertion point to the next field. Repeat the above procedure, as necessary. (If you don't want to enter data in a given field, press Enter as often as necessary until the insertion point is in the correct field.)

Handwriting data

To use handwriting recognition for the first time, you have to perform a custom install. Do this in the usual way but select Office Shared Features/Alternative User Input in Office's installer.

You can handwrite data into a writing pad and have Access convert it into standard text. You can also enter data via a virtual keyboard.

1 If the Language Bar isn't visible or minimised on the Taskbar, go to Control Panel. Double-click Text Services. In the dialog, click Language Bar. Select Show the Language bar on the desktop. Click OK twice. Now maximise the Language Bar, if necessary

You can import handwritten notes made on a Handheld or Pocket PC into Access – see the device's documentation.

2 Click Handwriting 3 Select Writing Pad

Language Bar

Re step 3 – click Write Anywhere to write directly on-screen, or On-Screen Standard Keyboard to use a virtual keyboard to enter text.

You can write with special devices (e.g. graphics tablets) or with the mouse.

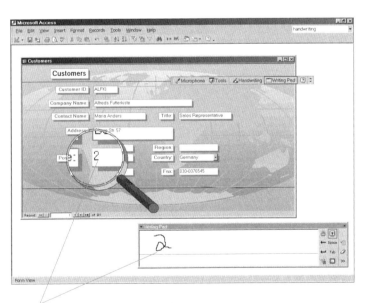

By default, Access converts data to text. However, you can have it entered as handwriting (which can be formatted in the normal way). Click this button in the Writing Pad:

4 Handwrite data on the line in the Writing Pad (don't pause between letters/digits but do leave appropriate spaces) – Access enters the data as soon as it recognizes it

Database navigation

Access 2002 makes it easy to move around in databases. The techniques for doing this are almost identical whether you're using Datasheet or Form views.

Using the Record Gauge

Press F5 to have Access 2002 place the insertion point in the Record Gauge. Then click any of the following locations to produce the specified effect:

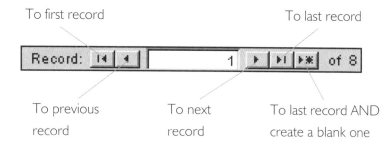

To first record

To last record

To previous record

To next record

To last record AND create a blank one

You can also jump to a record by carrying out the following procedure in the Gauge:

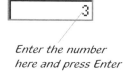

Enter the number here and press Enter

Using keyboard shortcuts

The following keystroke combinations can be used to move around in both Datasheet and Form views:

End	Moves to the last field in the current record
Home	Moves to the first field in the current record
Ctrl+End	Moves to the last field in the last record
Ctrl+Home	Moves to the first field in the first record
↑	(In Datasheet view and tables only) goes to the active field in the previous record
↓	(In Datasheet view and tables only) goes to the active field in the next record
Ctrl+ ↑	Moves to the active field in the first record
Ctrl+ ↓	Moves to the active field in the last record

In Form view, ↑ *moves to the previous field in the same record, and* ↓ *takes you to the next field in the same record.*

In Form view, Page Up and Page Down are subject to a proviso. When the start or end of the current record has been reached, Access 2002 moves to the previous or next record, respectively.

Page Up	Moves up by one screen
Page Down	Moves down by one screen
F5	Places the insertion point in the Record Gauge. (See the 'Using the Record Gauge' section on page 103 for how to use this.)
Ctrl+Page Up	(In Datasheet view) Moves one screen to the left
Ctrl+Page Down	(In Datasheet view) Moves one screen to the right

Using the scroll bars

In Datasheet view, you can use the horizontal scroll bar to move through fields which aren't currently visible. The vertical scroll bar moves through records which are currently off-screen:

In Form view, Ctrl+Page Up takes you to the previous record, and Ctrl+Page Down to the next.

As with all Windows programs, Access 2002 only displays scroll bars if the contents of a window are too large to display in their entirety.

Vertical scroll bar

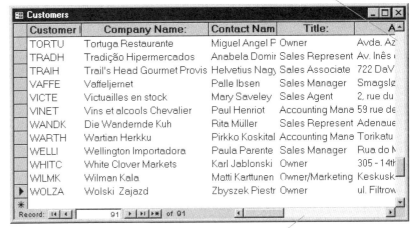

Horizontal scroll bar

In forms viewed in Form view, the scroll bars move you to hidden areas of the current record.

Amending data

To edit existing database data, click the appropriate field in the relevant record (this applies to both Datasheet and Form views). One of two things happens now:

- if the field is empty, you can begin typing in data immediately

- if the field already contains data, Access highlights it:

You can use Navigation mode in Form and Datasheet views.

In tables, you can use Navigation mode to inspect the details of hyperlinks without activating them.
Right-click over a hyperlink, then press Esc. Press F2 – the result looks something like this:

#FORMAGGI.HTM#

(This is a simple hyperlink pointing to a file – see page 113 for more information on hyperlinks.)

First Name    Karl

Simply begin typing; Access 2002 automatically overwrites the existing data

Entering Navigation mode

Access 2002 has a special mode which lets you move around *within* fields. Navigation mode is useful (even essential) if the field contents are extensive.

When Navigation mode is active, the various keystroke combinations work as they would normally in respect of text entry in a word processor. For example, the up and down cursor keys move the insertion point up or down within the field (rather than to the previous or next fields). Home moves the insertion point to the start of the current line, rather than taking it to the start of the current record; End takes it to the end of the current line, rather than taking it to the final field in the current record.

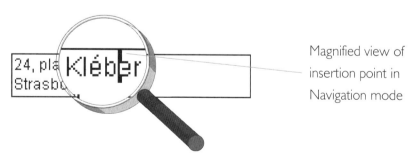

Magnified view of insertion point in Navigation mode

To enter Navigation mode, click a field and press F2. To return to data entry mode, press F2 again.

Access 2002 has another, particularly useful feature which you can use when the contents of a specific field exceed its width.

Using the Zoom box

The Zoom box is, in effect, a special editing window which displays the whole of a field's contents, however extensive.

The next illustration shows the field detail section of an address field in a database form:

Brecon House
Fifth Floor

You can use the Zoom box in Form and Datasheet views.

The address here consists of three lines, but only two display in the form. To view and/or edit the entire field, click in it. Then press Shift+F2. Now carry out the following steps:

| Type in replacement data, or click outside the highlighted text and make any necessary revisions

To turn on multiple language editing, click the Windows Start button. Select Programs, Microsoft Office Tools, Microsoft Office XP Language Settings. In the dialog, select an installed Office version, then the new language(s) you want to use. Click Add followed by OK.

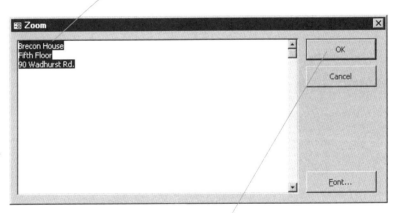

2 Click here

Spell-checking data

Access 2002 replaces some words/phrases automatically as you type (e.g. 'mkae' becomes 'make'). This is called AutoCorrect, and works with multiple languages (if you've set up Office to work with them – see the HOT TIP on the facing page).

To add your own substitutions, pull down the Tools menu and click AutoCorrect. In the Replace field, insert the incorrect word; in the With field, type in the correct one. Click OK.

Access makes use of two separate dictionaries. One – CUSTOM.DIC – is yours. When you click the Add button (see the tip below), the flagged word is stored in CUSTOM.DIC and recognised in future checking sessions.

If you're correcting a spelling error, you have two further options:

- *Click Add to have the flagged word stored in CUSTOM.DIC (see above), or;*

- *Click Change All to have Access substitute its suggestion for all future instances of the word*

Spell-checking a form or table

1 Open a form or table

2 In the case of data in Datasheet view, select the record(s), column(s), field(s) or text you want to check. In the case of Form view, select the field or text you want to check

3 Pull down the Tools menu and do the following:

4 Click Spelling

5 If one of the suggestions here is correct, click it, then follow step 6

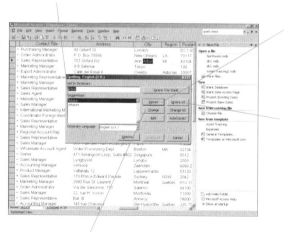

7 Click Ignore to ignore just this instance

8 Click Ignore All to ignore all future instances

6 Click Change to replace this instance

Deleting records

It's sometimes necessary to remove unwanted records from databases. Access 2002 makes this easy, in Datasheet or Form views.

In Form view, use the techniques listed in earlier topics to move to the record you want to delete. In forms or tables in Datasheet view, do the following:

Record header

The arrow (shown in a magnified view) is the record selector.

If you want to delete multiple records, you can only do so in Datasheet view.

Hold down Shift as you click the record headers at the start and end of the range of records you want to delete. Then follow steps 2-4.

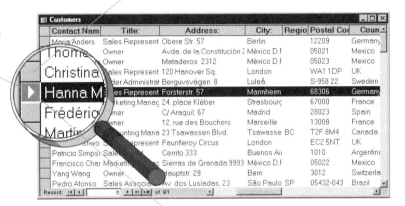

1 Click the appropriate entry in the Record header

2 Pull down the Edit menu and click Delete Record. Access 2002 launches a warning message. Do one of the following:

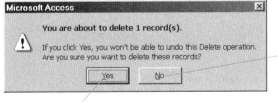

Record deletions are fixed: they can't be undone.

4 Click No to abort the deletion

3 Click Yes to delete the record(s)

Using Undo and Redo

From within Design view, Access lets you reverse – 'undo' – just about any editing operation. If, subsequently, you decide that you do want to proceed with an operation that you've reversed, you can 'redo' it. You can even undo or redo a series of operations in one go.

You can undo and redo actions in the following ways (in descending order of complexity):

To redo an action, carry out the following action on the Form Design toolbar:

Click here; in the list, select a redo action (but the HOT TIP below also applies).

- via the keyboard

- from within the Edit menu

- via a toolbar

Using the keyboard
Simply press Ctrl+Z to undo an action, or Ctrl+Y to reinstate it.

Using the Edit menu
Pull down the Edit menu and click Undo... or Redo... as appropriate (the ellipses denote the precise nature of the action to be reversed or reinstated).

Using the Form Design toolbar
Carry out the following action to undo an action (see the DON'T FORGET tip for how to reinstate it):

You can undo (but not redo) actions when you're inserting or amending records in Form or Datasheet view, but only one at a time.

(If you're using the toolbar route, refer to the Form View or Table Datasheet toolbar instead and simply click the Undo icon – there is no arrow.)

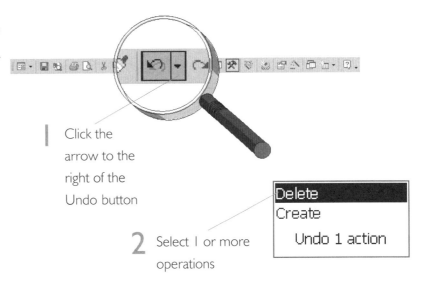

Click the arrow to the right of the Undo button

2 Select 1 or more operations

Delete
Create
Undo 1 action

Re step 2 – if you select an early operation in the list (i.e. one near the bottom), all later operations are included.

Find operations

If you want to restrict the search to a specific field in every record, select the field before you launch the Edit menu. Then select it in step 2.

Filters also represent a way to only view specific data.

If you need to find-and-replace data in bulk, consider using an update query instead – see chapter 7.

To locate unformatted blank fields, type in 'Null' (no quotes) in step 1 and untick Search Fields As Formatted.

To make searches case-specific, tick Match Case:

If you want to find or replace data in a subdatasheet, click in it before following the procedures here.

Access 2002 lets you search the active database for text and/or numbers. You can:

- search through all fields within every record, or limit the search to a specific field in every record

- search forwards or backwards, or through the whole database

- limit the search to exact matches (i.e. Access 2002 will only flag data which has the same upper- and lowercase make-up). For instance, a case-specific search for 'man' will not flag 'Man' or 'MAN'

- limit the search to 'match types' (the beginning of fields, the whole field or any part) – see step 4 below

Searching for data

Pull down the Edit menu and click Find. Now carry out step 1 below, then steps 2–4, as appropriate. (Additionally, see the HOT TIPS for other ways to customise the search.) Finally, carry out step 5:

1 Type in the data you want to find

2 Click here; select a field or datasheet/form to search

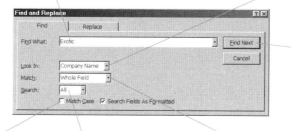

5 Click here to flag the next match

3 Click here; select a search direction (Up, Down or All)

4 Click here; select a match type

Repeat step 4 as necessary to locate further instances of the data specified in step 1.

Find-and-replace operations

If you want to restrict the search to a specific field in every record, select the field before you launch the Edit menu. Then select it in step 3.

When you search for data you can also – if you want – have Access 2002 replace it with something else. You can:

- search through all fields within every record, or limit the search to a specific field in every record

- search forwards or backwards, or through the whole database

- limit the search to exact matches (i.e. Access 2002 will only flag data which has the same upper- and lowercase make-up)

Replacing data

Pull down the Edit menu and click Replace. Perform steps 1–2, then 3–4 if relevant. Now do one of the following:

Re step 1 on pages 110 and 111 – you can also enter wildcards:

? stands for any 1 character

* stands for any number of characters

For instance, searching for 'wh?le' (the quotes are merely for emphasis) will find 'whole' or 'while', and 'wh?le*' will also locate 'wholesome'.

- Follow step 5. When Access 2002 locates the first search target, carry out step 6 to have it replaced. Repeat as often as required

- Carry out step 7 to have *every* target replaced automatically

1 Type in the data you want to find

2 Type in replacement data

5 Click here to flag the 1st occurrence

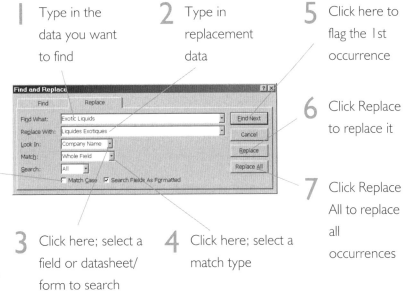

If you need to make searches case-specific, tick Match Case:

6 Click Replace to replace it

7 Click Replace All to replace all occurrences

3 Click here; select a field or datasheet/form to search

4 Click here; select a match type

To specify a search direction, click in the Search field and select Up, Down or All.

Sorting data

In forms and tables in Datasheet view, you can sort by more than one field (from the left, but only in the same sort order). Simply select more than one column before you sort.

To return your data to the way it was before a sort, choose Records, Remove Filter/Sort.

You can perform more complex sorts (e.g. one field Ascending and one Descending). Launch the Advanced Filter/Sort dialog (see page 114) from any form, table or query. Complete more than 1 column (Access sorts from the left) in the Design grid but omit the criteria. Choose Filter, Apply Filter/Sort.

In a table (in Datasheet view) or a form (in Design view) you can create hyperlinks to e-mail addresses.

Press Ctrl+K (in tables, you must be in a field to which you've applied the Hyperlink data type). In the dialog that launches, click E-Mail Address under Link to:. Complete the rest of the dialog. Click OK.

Find operations locate specific records based on one specified criterion. However, Access 2002 lets you take this a stage further. You can have records arranged in a specific order; this is called 'sorting'. Sorting your data often helps you find information more quickly, in both tables and forms. You can sort data in ascending order, with the following level of priority:

- 0 to 9

then

- A to Z

You can also sort data in descending order (9 to 0, Z to A).

Carrying out a sort

In either Datasheet or Form view, click the field on which you want to base the sort. Pull down the Records menu and click Sort, Sort Ascending or Sort, Sort Descending.

Before the sort...

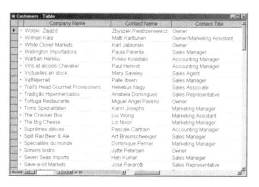

...after a descending sort has been applied to the Company Name field on the far left

Hyperlinks

You can type in a web address as a hyperlink, or you can use an expanded syntax:

displaytext#address#screentip

'Displaytext' is (optional) text which displays in the field itself; 'address' is self-explanatory and essential; 'screentip' is (optional) extra text which appears when you hold the mouse pointer over the hyperlink.

An example (but omit the breaks):

Computer Step's website#http://www.ineasysteps.com# a great place for books!

To amend a hyperlink, right-click it. Choose Hyperlink, Edit Hyperlink (or Hyperlink, Remove Hyperlink to delete it) and complete the dialog which launches.

To use a hyperlink in a form, ensure you're in Form view. Move the mouse pointer over the hyperlink – the cursor becomes a pointing hand:

This jumps to a local Access database

Left-click once.

You can use hyperlinks in tables or forms to jump to:

- another Access 2002 database

- a site on the Internet

Inserting a hyperlinked field into a table

Follow the procedures on page 62 to open the relevant table in Design view. Then follow steps 2–4 on page 65 to set up and classify a new field. (In step 4, however, select Hyperlink as the data type.) Go to Datasheet view; in the hyperlinked field entry which corresponds to the appropriate record, type in details of the specific hyperlink. (See the DON'T FORGET tip on the left for clarification):

A table hyperlink to a website – 'visible text' is displaying (in blue)

Using a hyperlink in a table

Ensure you're in Datasheet view. Move the mouse pointer over the entry you want to jump to (the cursor changes to a pointing hand). Left-click once.

Inserting a hyperlink into a form

First, follow the procedures on page 88 to open the relevant form in Design view. Then click this button – 🖳 – in the Form Design toolbar. In the Insert Hyperlink dialog, select Existing File or Web Page. In the Address field, type in the address of the file or Internet site you want to jump to. Click OK. Access inserts the relevant hyperlink:

http://www.ineasysteps.com

Move and/or resize this using standard Windows techniques.

Filtering data

This method produces complex filters. Two simpler methods you can use are:

Filter by Selection	You select a value – Access only returns records which match it
Filter by Form	A version of the active datasheet or form launches – you complete the relevant empty fields to have Access match these

Select these from the Records, Filter menu.

Sorting data is one way of customising the way it displays on screen. Another method you can use is 'filtering'. When you apply a filter, Access 2002 temporarily hides records which don't match the requirements ('criteria') you set.

Filtering involves:

- selecting the fields through which Access 2002 should search

- specifying the sort order (one particular advantage to filtering is that you can apply differing sort orders to the various fields)

- specifying what the fields must contain ('criteria') to have their records display

- applying the filter

Setting up a filter

In Datasheet or Form view, pull down the Records menu and click Filter, Advanced Filter/Sort – the Advanced Filter/Sort dialog launches. Do the following:

Repeat steps 1-4 for as many fields as you want to include in the filter.

Note that Access may pre-select a field and insert it in the first column. If this isn't what you want, click the arrow to the right of the Field box and select the correct field from the list. Then follow steps 2–3.

1 | Double-click a field to have it appear in the Field box

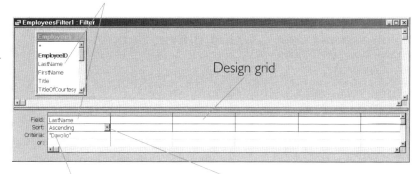

Design grid

Re step 3 – criteria are usually simple to use. For instance, in the example shown, the first field pulls in records whose LastName entry is 'Davolio'.

3 Type in criteria in the Criteria field

2 Click the arrow on the right of the Sort field – in the list, select Ascending or Descending

When you filter data, the effects are only temporary: the underlying table is unaffected.

Another way to apply a filter is to click the following button:

in the Filter/Sort, Form View or Table Datasheet toolbars.

Removing a filter does not delete it: it just makes it inactive, so that all records now display.
(Removal also affects filters created in any subdatasheets within the host datasheet.)

Queries are similar in function to filters, in that they both sort records. However, use queries if you need to:

* *specify which fields from the source records display*
* *choose which tables you want to work with*

Applying a filter

Once you've set up a filter, the next stage is to implement it.

1 With the Advanced Filter/Sort dialog active, pull down the Filter menu and do the following

2 Click here

Removing a filter

When you've finished with a filter, you can deactivate it.

1 With the form or datasheet active, pull down the Records menu and do the following:

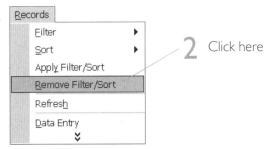

2 Click here

Deleting a filter

When you've finished with a filter, you can erase it.

1 Click in the form or datasheet in which you created the filter

2 In the Records menu, select Filter, Advanced Filter/Sort

3 In the Edit menu, select Clear Grid, then follow steps 1–2 under 'Applying a filter'

Saving/opening filters

Access 2002 regards filters as queries. For how to work with queries, see Chapter 7.

Filters created in a query are also saved with the query, but the criteria aren't. Re-enter them when you load the query.

Saved filters appear as queries under the Queries tab in the Database window.

When you save the host form or table, details of any filter you've set up are also saved. You can reapply the filters when you reopen the form/table. However, it's a good idea to save filters as separate queries. This makes them readily accessible in other tables, forms or queries.

Saving a filter as a query

With the Advanced Filter/Sort dialog still open, pull down the File menu and click Save As Query. Do the following:

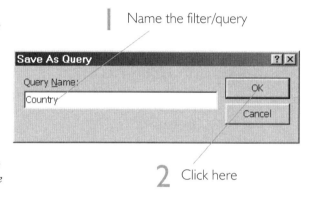

Name the filter/query

2 Click here

Reopening a filter

To work with a filter you've already set up, make sure the Advanced Filter dialog is open. Pull down the File menu and click Load From Query. Do the following:

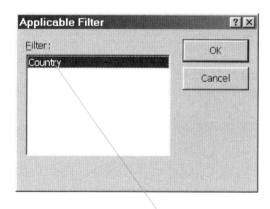

Double-click the relevant filter

Using speech recognition

Dictating data into Access 2002 provides a valuable alternative way to input it – you can also use speech recognition to enter commands etc.

First, you'll carry out a custom install, to install speech recognition for use with Access. Then you'll 'train' the software, so it's set up for your voice and dictating conditions. You'll go on to dictate content into Access 2002 and have it turned into on-screen data. When errors occur, you'll correct them with the mouse and keyboard (in the usual way) or dictate the replacement.

Finally, you'll launch menus, toolbar buttons, dialogs and the Task Pane with dedicated voice commands.

Covers

Chapter Six

Preparing to use speech recognition

To use speech recognition, you need the following:

- a high-quality headset, preferably with USB (Universal Serial Bus) support and gain adjustment

- a minimum chip speed of 400 MHz (slower chips make dictation extremely laborious)

- a minimum of 128 Mb of RAM

- Windows 98 (or NT 4.0) or later

- Internet Explorer 5.0 (or later)

For more information on requirements, visit (no spaces or line breaks):

http://office.microsoft.com/ assistance/2002/articles/ oSpeechRequirements_aw.htm

The Microphone Wizard only launches the first time you follow step 1 (after this, step 1 activates speech recognition).

Your use of speech recognition will benefit from repeated training. Click the Tools button on the Language Bar and select Training. Complete the wizard which launches.

Installing/running speech recognition

If you haven't already done so, you must first run a custom install. In Control Panel, double-click Add/Remove Programs. Select Microsoft Office XP... Click Add/Remove, then Add or Remove Features, Next. Double-click Office Shared Features, then Alternative User Input. Select Speech then the type of installation you need. Click Update.

Preparing speech recognition

Before you can dictate into Access 2002, you have to adjust your microphone and carry out a brief 'training' procedure to acclimatise Access to the sound of your voice:

1 Choose Tools, Speech

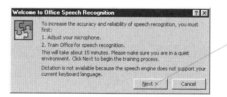

2 Click Next to begin the training process

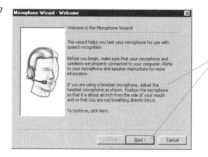

3 Adjust your microphone in line with the instructions then click Next

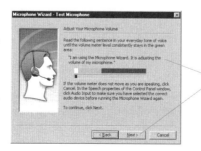

4 Read out the sentence shown then click Next. Complete the rest of the wizard – it should take about 15 minutes

Dictating data

If you run speech recognition in less than optimal

conditions, the results may well be poor.

To get the best out of speech recognition, you need to carry out the

following:

- *keep your environment as quiet as possible*

- *keep the microphone in the same position relative to your mouth*

- *run the training wizard as often as possible*

- *pronounce words clearly but don't pause between them or between individual letters – only pause at the end of your train of thought*

- *turn off the microphone when not in use (by repeating step 1)*

For the best results, use speech recognition in conjunction

with mouse and keyboard use.

1 Follow step 1 on page 118

2 If the microphone isn't already turned on, click here

3 The Language bar expands – click Dictation

4 Begin dictating. Initially, Access inserts a blue bar on the screen – the data/text appears as soon as it's recognised:

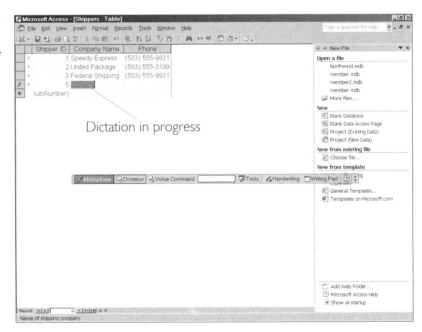

Dictation in progress

5 To close speech recognition when you've finished, repeat step 1

Entering voice commands

You can switch to Voice Command by saying 'Voice Command', or dictation by saying 'Dictation'.

| Follow step 1 on page 118

2 Click Voice Command

Commands you speak appear in the following Language bar field:

Task Pane

3 Issue the appropriate command using the following as guides:

*   to launch the File menu say 'file' or 'file menu' (to select a menu entry say the name)
*   to open the Font dialog say 'font' (to select a typeface, say the name)
*   to close a dialog say 'OK'
*   to select a toolbar button, say the name
*   to launch the New File Task Pane, say 'file' then 'new'

For more details of voice commands, see the HELP topic 'Getting started with speech recognition'.

Correcting errors

If the Language Bar isn't visible or minimised on the Taskbar, go to Control Panel. Double-click Text Services. In the dialog, click Language Bar. Select Show the Language bar on the desktop. Click OK twice.

| Replace wrong text with corrections in the usual way

2 Or select the error with your mouse . In Dictation mode, say 'spelling mode'. Pause, then spell out the substitution e.g. o-n-c-e

3 Or select the error with your mouse (it's best to also select one or two correct words on either side of the error). In Dictation mode, say the words you selected

Re step 3 – it's best to correct phrases rather than individual words.

Querying databases

This chapter shows you how to retrieve highly specific information from your databases with the use of sophisticated queries. You'll learn how to create Select, Crosstab, Update and Parameter queries rapidly, some with wizards and others manually.

Finally, you'll save your query to disk, and then discover how to open and apply it.

Covers

Chapter Seven

Queries – an overview

You can also generate Update queries. These make amendments to multiple records in one or more tables.

First, follow the procedures under 'Creating a query manually' later to create a query which contains the relevant tables and queries. With the query still open in Design view, click the arrow to the right of this button on the toolbar:

In the menu, select Update Query. Now refer to the Field list – drag the fields you want to update onto the Design grid. Specify any relevant criteria then, in the Update To box relating to the fields you want to update, type in updated values. Finally, click this toolbar button to action the query:

Before running an Update query, backup your data so you can restore it, if necessary.

In Chapter 5, we looked at ways to enter data into databases. However, a large part of database use consists of extracting information. The trick is to get precisely the information you need, in the right format. Queries represent a highly accurate and useful way of doing this.

When you set up and institute a query, you 'interrogate' the active database; the result – the 'answer' – can then be viewed on screen, or even printed. At the same time, the information which does not satisfy the criteria you set is conveniently ignored, although of course it still remains within the database. The ability to (in effect) hide information is what makes queries so indispensable.

The main types of query are:

Select queries	These extract information from tables, based on the criteria you specify. Select queries are the most frequent type, and the Access 2002 default.
Crosstab queries	These use criteria you set to summarise table data in a spreadsheet format. Crosstab queries are the most complex to use, but arguably the most useful.

Query creation

You can create queries in two ways:

- with Query Wizards

- manually

There are four Query Wizards; we'll examine two (the Simple Query and Crosstab Query Wizards) in some detail in this chapter.

We'll also look at manual query creation.

The Simple Query Wizard

You can also create Parameter queries. These launch dialogs which you can complete to apply the query.

First, follow the procedures under 'Creating a query manually' to create a query which contains the relevant tables and queries. With the query still open in Design view, refer to the Criteria box for the field you want to use as a parameter and type in the relevant expression, using the following as a guideline:

<[Units available:]

When you run the query, a dialog appears:

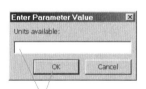

Enter a value & confirm

Re step 3 – you can run two other wizards here. The Find Duplicates Query Wizard locates records with duplicated field values in any one table; the Find Unmatched Query Wizard compares tables and isolates records which are unrelated.

To run either of these, simply double-click the relevant entry and follow the on-screen instructions.

Use the Simple Query Wizard to create a Select query.

First, make sure the Database window is visible. Then do the following:

1 Ensure Queries is activated

2 Click the New button

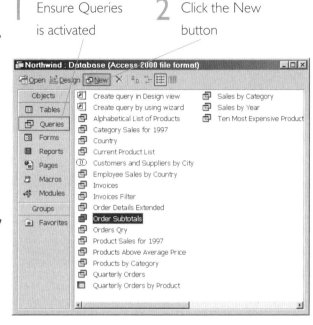

3 Double-click Simple Query Wizard

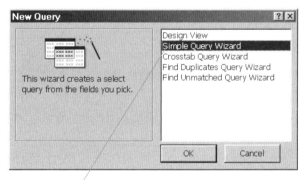

See Chapter 11 for how to print queries.

If you want to use fields from additional tables or queries, repeat steps 4–5.

You can base queries on a filter you've created and saved as a query.

4 Click here; select a table or query in the list

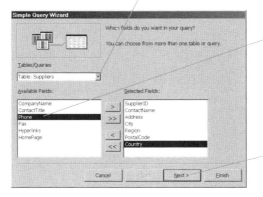

5 Double-click the field(s) you want to include in the query

6 Click here

7 Name the query

8 Click here to open the new query after step 9

9 Click here

The end result:

The query displays in Datasheet view.

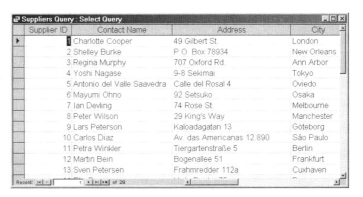

The Crosstab Query Wizard

With Crosstab queries, information is grouped by two data types, one on the left of the datasheet and the other along the top.

Crosstab queries summarise data from the fields you specify, and present it in a convenient tabular form.

Follow steps 1–3 on page 123 (in 3, however, double-click Crosstab Query Wizard)

Re step 2 – click Queries instead if you want to base the new query on an existing one. Select this in step 3, then follow the remaining steps.

In this example, we take two fields from a database relating to a music collection:

- *Recording Title*
- *Recording Artist ID*

Then we instruct the Crosstab Query wizard (in later dialogs) to correlate the total number of tracks (the 'correlation field') in each title against the appropriate Artist ID number...

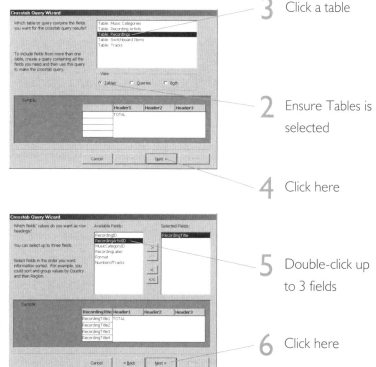

3 Click a table

2 Ensure Tables is selected

4 Click here

5 Double-click up to 3 fields

6 Click here

This section: previews your selected fields.

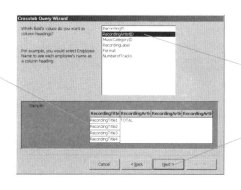

7 Click the field you want to serve as the column heading

8 Click here

Access 2002 previews the resultant query here:

9 Click a correlation field (see the DON'T FORGET tip on page 125)

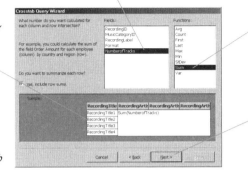

10 Click a calculation type

11 Click here

You can also create Crosstab queries from scratch, in Design view. However, the wizard provides a much easier route...

12 Name the query

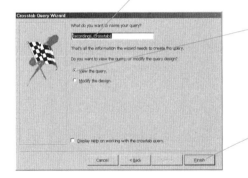

13 Ensure this is selected to open the new query after step 14

14 Click here

The end result:

Artists' ID numbers

Recording Title	Total Of Numbe	1	2	3	4
Look Both Way	12		12		
Meditations	6				6
Noise in the Ga	10		10		
Opus 65	5	5			
Outback	10		10		
Short Circuit	7			7	
Sounds Better L	10		10		

Individual track totals

Creating a query manually

Follow steps 1–3 on page 123 (but in 3 double-click Design View)

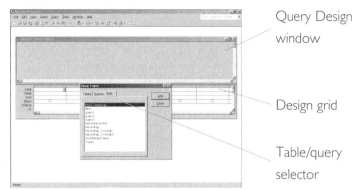

Query Design window

Design grid

Table/query selector

When you add more than 1 table to a query, you must tell Access 2002 how their fields interrelate. You do this by linking their field lists via join lines.

Access 2002 establishes join lines when the following conditions are met:

- *when it detects that two fields have a compatible data type, and;*
- *when one is a primary key*

If no join lines are established, you should rectify this – see page 128. (If you don't do this, every record combination displays, a case of information overload.)

The next stage is to select the tables (and/or existing queries) which contain the fields you want to insert into your query.

2 Ensure this tab is active

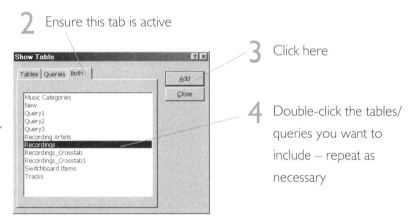

3 Click here

4 Double-click the tables/ queries you want to include – repeat as necessary

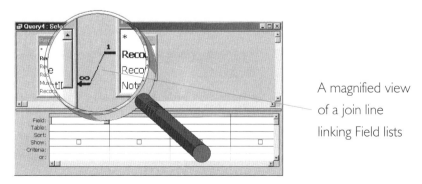

A magnified view of a join line linking Field lists

You can specify the type of join used (e.g. you can elect to exclude rows whose joined fields are unequal).

Right-click the join line. In the menu, click Join Properties. In the Join Properties dialog, select a join type then click OK.

The next stage is to join tables in the Design window if:

- you have more than one Field list in the window

- the Field lists relate to tables (they probably will)

- Access hasn't already created a valid automatic join (see the HOT TIP on page 127 for more on this)

Do the following:

You can display queries in two views: Datasheet view and Design view. Datasheet view shows the result of applying the query whereas Design view (as here) is used to customise it. Use Datasheet view as a way of previewing your query before you run it (but not in Update queries).

5 Click a field; drag it to its counterpart in the second table

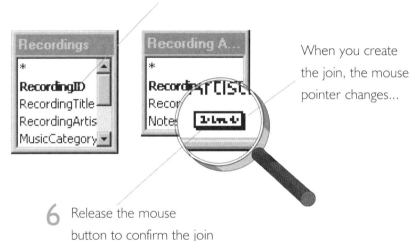

When you create the join, the mouse pointer changes...

6 Release the mouse button to confirm the join

The illustration below shows the completed join:

Join line (here, a one-to-many relationship)

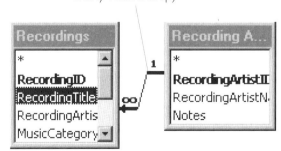

Re step 7 – as you double-click subsequent fields, Access 2002 inserts them in adjacent columns in the Design grid (as here).

Now carry out the following steps:

7 Double-click a field

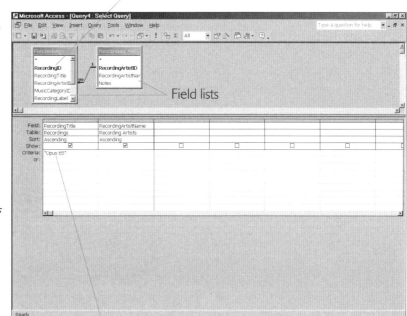

Field lists

Re step 8 – criteria are usually simple to use. For instance, in this example the first field pulls in records where the track title is 'Opus 65'. The second field displays the associated Recording Artist.

To apply a query in Design view, pull down the Query menu and click Run. Or click this button:

8 Type in criteria (and – optionally – choose a sort order)

Repeat steps 7–8 for as many fields (using all the relevant Field lists in the Query Design window) as you want to include in the query.

The final stage in creating a manual query is to save it to disk for future use. See page 132 how to do this.

in the Query Design toolbar.

Viewing queries interactively

You can view queries in a way which lets you interact dynamically with them. This allows you to analyse your data on-the-fly.

Displaying queries in PivotTable view

1 On the left of the database window, select Queries

2 On the right of the database window, double-click a query

3 Pull down the View menu and select PivotTable view

To stop a query, press the Ctrl+Break keys.

4 Drag any of the fields in the Field List window to the appropriate PivotTable area – see page 86 for guidelines on how to do this

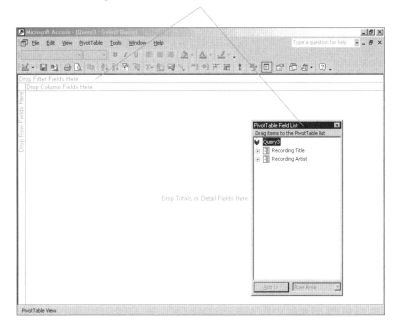

5 In the completed PivotTable, you can drag any of the fields to new locations (or add new ones) and the data will update. You can also filter the PivotTable by clicking any of the arrows to the right of the fields and deselecting entries

Displaying queries in PivotChart view

1 On the left of the database window, select Queries

2 On the right of the database window, double-click a query

3 Pull down the View menu and select PivotChart view

4 Drag any of the fields in the Field List window to the appropriate PivotChart area – see page 86 for guidelines on how to do this

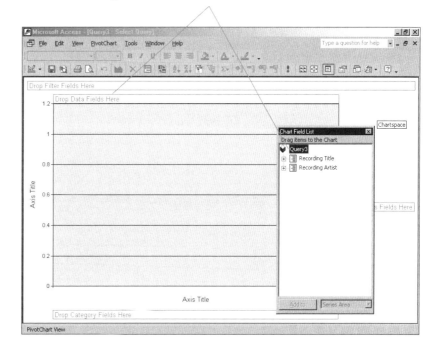

5 In the completed PivotChart, you can drag any of the fields to new locations (or add new ones) and the data will update. You can also filter the PivotTable by clicking any of the arrows to the right of the fields and deselecting entries

Saving your query

Manually generated queries need to be saved to disk for later use.

Saving a query

With the Query Design window still open, pull down the File menu and do the following:

To open a query, press F11. On the left of the Database window, select Queries. Double-click any query on the right.

When you open a manual query you've previously saved to disk, Access 2002 applies it to your data. (However, queries created with a wizard are automatically opened and applied at the end of the creation process – see earlier topics for more information on this.)

If you want to amend existing queries, press F11. On the left of the Database window, select Queries. Select a query on the right and click Design in the toolbar. Now amend the query via the techniques discussed earlier.

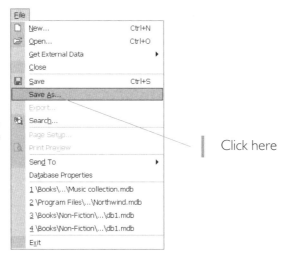

Click here

2 Name the query

3 Click here

Creating reports

Here, you'll view your data in printed format, as reports. You'll learn how to create less complex AutoReports then build advanced reports with the Report Wizard. You'll go on to create and sort reports manually (for more precision) and customise the way report components display, so your data is presented just the way you want it. Finally, you'll create subreports, labels, hyperlinks and report 'snapshots' (so non-Access users can view them); AutoFormat your reports; preview them; save your manually generated reports to disk; and then reopen them.

Covers

Chapter Eight

Reports – an overview

In Chapter 4, we looked at the creation and use of database forms. Forms allow you to enter data in a user-friendly way. Reports have a similar effect on the way you view (and print) data. When you create and view a report, however, you have:

- more control over the layout

- the ability to customise the printed output (see Chapter 11 for more information on printing reports)

Reports can be based on either tables, queries or instances of both, but don't have to contain all of their fields.

Before you set up and institute a report, you should do the following:

1. examine your database, taking account of the current tables, forms and queries

2. be clear in your own mind which components of your database represent data, and make sure you've entered all the data you want reports to display

3. if you want to enter data as well as view it, use a form (you can't enter information into reports)

Reports display data in a printed format.

4. if you've created previous reports (or if you've used a wizard to create a database and reports have been created automatically in the process, as is normally the case), review them with a view to highlighting areas which need improving

Report creation

You can create reports in three ways:

- with AutoReports

- with the Report Wizard

- manually

Wizards/AutoReports

The three principal ways to automate report creation are:

You can create subreports (reports within reports). In the Toolbox, ensure this icon is depressed:

Click this button:

In the report, click where you want to insert the subreport. The Subreport Wizard launches; complete the various dialogs, clicking Next when appropriate to move on to subsequent ones. In the final dialog, click Finish to complete the subreport.

Columnar AutoReport   Automatically creates a quick, simple report for the selected table in a single column

Tabular AutoReport   As above, but creates the report in a tabular format

Report Wizard   Provides full control over which tables and fields are included, and extensive customisation

The AutoReports are an especially quick and convenient way to create reports. Use the Report Wizard when you need greater precision.

Columnar AutoReport

Tabular AutoReport

Creating AutoReport reports

Use the AutoReport route to report creation when you want to create a report based on a single table or query. With AutoReports, all the underlying fields display.

Re step 3 – Access 2002 provides an extra Report Wizard: the Label Wizard. This creates reports which produce highly customisable labels in various formats.

To run the Label Wizard, double-click its name in the New Report dialog box and follow the on-screen instructions.

In reports created with AutoReport, note the following facts:

- *all fields/records in the base table/query display*
- *each field appears on a separate line*

To create a single-column report, open a table or query. Do the following in the toolbar:

Click here; in the list, select AutoReport

First, make sure the Database window is visible. Now carry out the following steps:

1 Ensure the Reports tab is activated

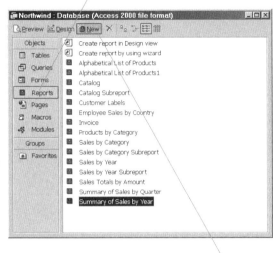

2 Click here

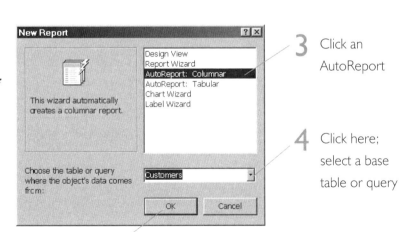

3 Click an AutoReport

4 Click here; select a base table or query

5 Click here – Access creates an AutoForm using the last AutoFormat you applied (if applicable) or the Standard AutoFormat (see page 144)

Using the Report Wizard

First, make sure the Database window is visible. Now carry out the following steps:

1 Follow steps 1–4 on page 136 (in 3, however, click Report Wizard) then click OK

Re step 2 – if you want to use fields from an additional table and/or query, click the arrow to the right of the Tables/Queries box. Make one or more selections from the list. Finally, double-click the relevant fields and carry out steps 3–5, as appropriate.

2 Double-click the field(s) you want to include

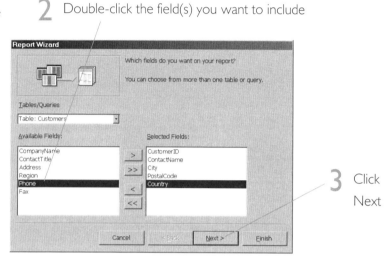

3 Click Next

Use the wizard route to report creation when you want to create a report based on more than one table or query.

In the next dialog, if any of the fields can be grouped under a convenient heading (this makes reports easier to follow), carry out steps 4 and 5 below (if not, simply follow step 5):

4 Double-click the heading field

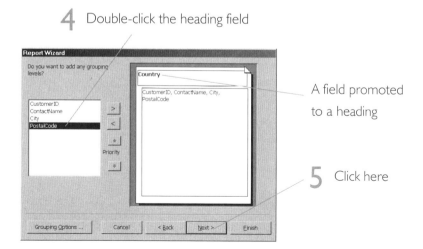

A field promoted to a heading

5 Click here

If you followed steps 4 AND 5 on page 137, you now allocate sort fields for 'detail records' (those organised under group headings). If, on the other hand, you defined no headings, you sort all records here.

To toggle between Ascending or Descending sorts, click the button to the right of each sort field.

In the next dialog you can select up to four sort fields as a basis for ordering records. Carry out steps 6–7 below (to allocate more than one sort field, repeat step 6 for fields below the first, THEN follow 7). Finally, follow steps 8–10:

6 Click the arrow then select a sort field

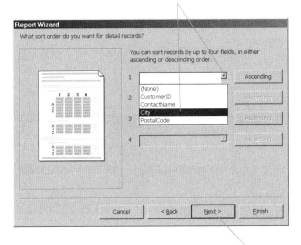

7 Click Next

8 Choose a report layout

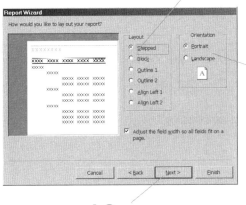

9 Choose a report orientation

10 Click Next

Now carry out the following steps:

| | Select a report style

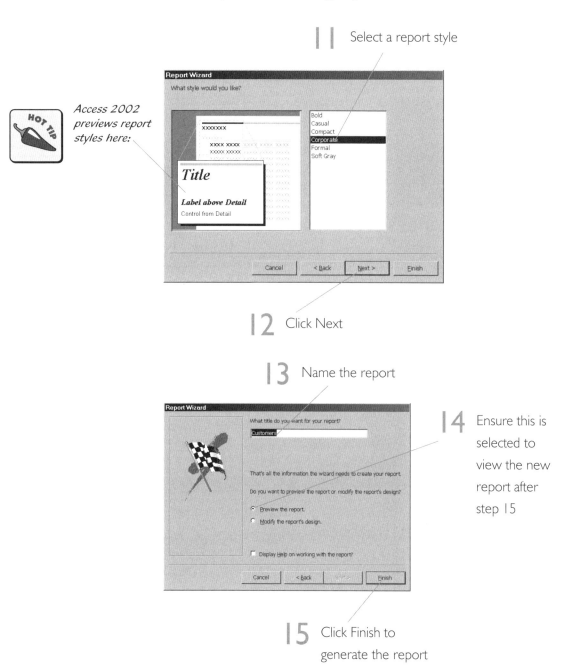

Access 2002 previews report styles here:

| 2 Click Next

| 3 Name the report

| 4 Ensure this is selected to view the new report after step | 5

| 5 Click Finish to generate the report

Creating reports manually

1 Follow steps 1–2 on page 136

Follow steps 1–2 on page 136

When you create a report without using a wizard, Access bases its structure on a template. You can nominate any report as this base template.

Pull down the Tools menu and click Options. In the Options dialog, select the Forms/Reports tab. In the Report template field, type the name of the new template and click OK.

2 Click Design View

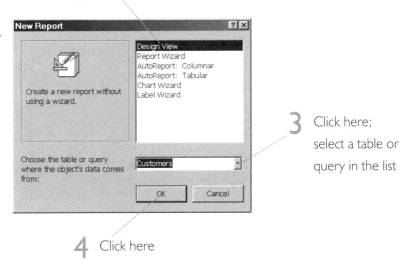

3 Click here; select a table or query in the list

4 Click here

5 After step 4, Access 2002 creates a blank report and launches the Field list:

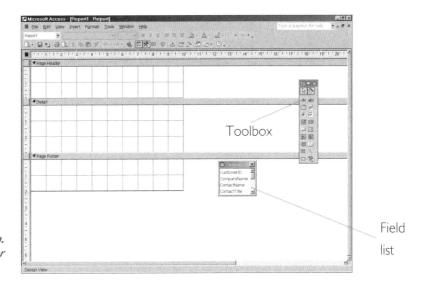

Toolbox

Field list

The report appears in Design view, ready for customisation.

(See pages 141–151 for how to customise the new report.)

Report design – an overview

If you want to, you can also opt to redesign reports created with the various wizards.

Now that you've created a report manually, you need to add the various fields and labels (explanatory text). As with forms, Access 2002 calls everything you add to a report a 'control'. There are two main types:

- bound

- unbound

Bound controls pull in data from fields in an underlying database table or query. For instance, if a field in a table contains Address information, the relevant control will return location data for the currently active record.

For how to preview your work at any stage in the report design process, see page 152.

Unbound controls, on the other hand, contain supplementary text (e.g. instructions to the database user) or graphics components (e.g. lines); they aren't connected to table fields.

The illustration below shows an excerpt from a previewed report:

Examples of labels
(unbound fields)

Alphabetical Member Listing

Member Name	Member Type	Work Phone
B		
John Bacon		
Art Braunschweiger	Full Member	(307) 555-4680
Steven Buchanan	Full Member	(71) 555-4848

Examples of
Bound fields

Amending report design

You can add hyperlinks to reports. To insert a hyperlink, follow the appropriate procedures here to open the report in Design view. Then click this button:

in the Report Design toolbar. In the Insert Hyperlink dialog, select Existing File or Web Page. In the Address field, type in the address of the file or Internet site you want to jump to. Click OK. Access inserts the relevant hyperlink

There are two ways to begin customising a report's design.

If the report is already open
Pull down the View menu and carry out the following step:

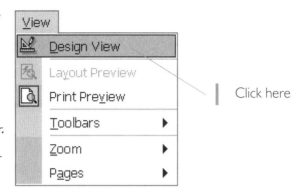

Click here

If the report isn't already open
Go to the Database window and do the following:

3 Click Design

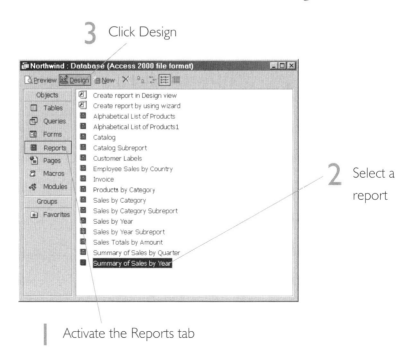

2 Select a report

Activate the Reports tab

If you've just created a manual report, you'll already be in Design View.

Access 2002 now launches the report in Design view. This is the basis for adding and customising fields. Design View's three principal components are shown below:

If the Field List or Toolbox aren't visible, pull down the View menu and click Field List or Toolbox respectively.

Detail pane   Field List

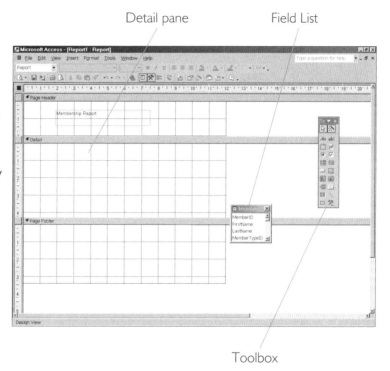

Toolbox

The Detail pane

The Detail pane represents the current body of your report. Here, you create and design the necessary fields. You can resize it as required:

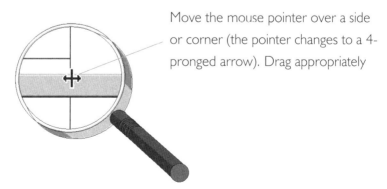

Move the mouse pointer over a side or corner (the pointer changes to a 4-pronged arrow). Drag appropriately

AutoFormat

You can apply a series of pre-defined formats to overall report design. Use AutoFormat to impose:

- a background

- a preset control font

- a preset control border

Using AutoFormat

With the relevant report open in Design View, do the following to select it:

If the Report Selector doesn't look like this:

click it

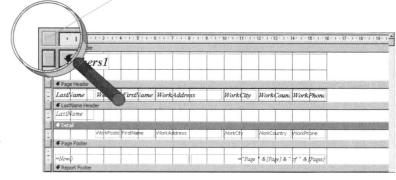

If you don't want to apply all 3 aspects of an AutoFormat, carry out step 2. Now click the Options button. Deselect:

- *Font*

- *Color*

- *Border*

(as appropriate) in the extended dialog. Finally, carry out step 3.

Now pull down the Format menu and click AutoFormat. Carry out the following steps:

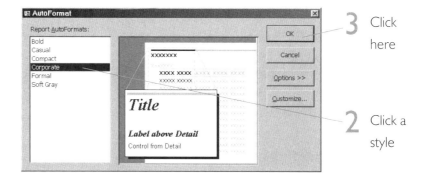

3 Click here

2 Click a style

Adding labels

Unlike forms, Access 2002 reports automatically display header and footer areas.

It's useful to add descriptive labels to reports. Report areas you can add labels to include:

- the report header or footer

- the Detail pane

First, refer to the Toolbox and do the following:

Re step 1 – if the Toolbox isn't visible, pull down the View menu and click Toolbox.

Click here

Here, the Detail pane is uncluttered because this is a manually created report. Detail panes for wizard-generated reports will be more complex.

2 Move the pointer to the appropriate location in the header/footer or Detail pane. Drag to define the label area:

You can define labels in the Page Header and Page Footer areas:

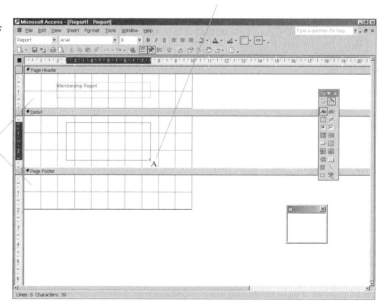

So far, your label will look something like this:

You can add tabbed controls to reports. To do this, click this button:

in the Toolbox. In the report, click where you want the tabbed control to go. This is the result:

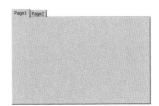

Label

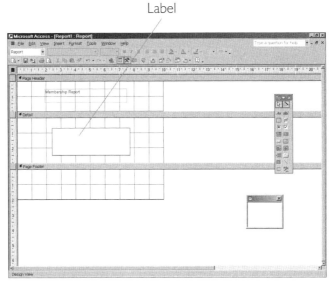

3 Type in the label text. When you've finished, press Enter

The end result:

The inserted label

You'll probably need to reformat most labels after you've created them.
(See pages 148–151 for how to do this.)

Adding fields

Re step 1 – if no fields appear in the Field list, the probable reason is that you omitted step 3 on page 140 when creating the report: as no underlying table or query was selected, there are no fields to choose from.

To solve this, right-click the Detail pane. In the menu, select Properties. Click in the field at the top of the dialog which appears and select Report. Activate the Data tab then click in the Record Source field – in the list, select a base table or query. Press Alt+F4 to close the dialog.

Once you've inserted the necessary labels, the next stage is to insert the required fields. This is a simple process which involves a drag-and-drop technique.

In Design view, make sure the Field List is visible. (If it isn't, pull down the View menu and click Field List.) Then do the following:

To add new (extra) fields to the Field List, open the table (in Datasheet view) which underlies the report. Follow the procedures in the HOT TIP on page 54 to add a new field. When you reopen the original report, the new field appears in the Field List.

Note that fields in reports consist of the following parts:

Member Type

The field name

MemberTypeID ▾

The field detail

| Drag a field to the appropriate location in the report

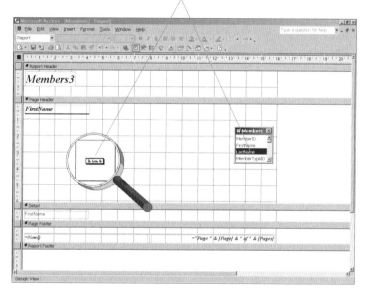

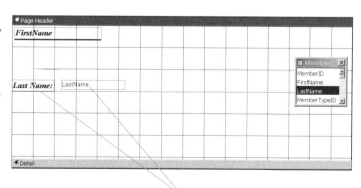

2 The new field is created – amend it as necessary

Reformatting labels and fields

If the Formatting (Form/Report) toolbar isn't on-screen, pull down the View menu and tick Toolbars, Formatting (Form/Report).

You can select multiple controls by holding down Shift as you click them.

Once you've inserted a new label or field, you can:

* apply a new typeface and/or type size

* align the contents

* apply foreground and/or background colours

* specify a border width and/or colour

* apply special effects

Applying a new typeface

With the relevant report open in Design View, select the control(s) you want to amend. Then refer to the Formatting (Form/Report) toolbar and do the following:

If you want to reformat the field name as well as the field detail, don't forget to select it, too.

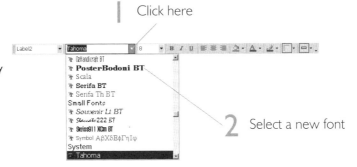

Applying a new type size

If you need greater precision, omit steps 1 and 2. Instead, type in a new type size here: Then press Return.

With the relevant report open in Design View, select the control(s) you want to amend. Then do the following:

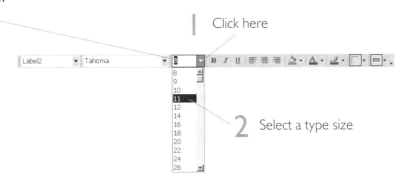

Aligning label and field contents

With the relevant report open in Design View, select the control(s) you want to amend. Then carry out step 1 to left-align the contents, step 2 to centre them or step 3 to right-align them:

See the following illustrations for brief details of alignment in action:

Title	Left
Title	Center
Title	Right

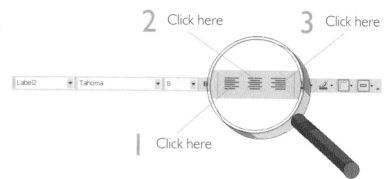

Colouring foregrounds and backgrounds

With the relevant report open in Design View, select the control(s) you want to amend. Then follow steps 1 AND 2 below to apply a background colour, or 3 AND 4 to apply a foreground colour:

To sort fields in a report while in Design view, pull down the View menu and click Sorting and Grouping. Click in the Field/Expression field in the Sorting and Grouping dialog; in the list, select the first sort field. Optionally, click in the field on the right and select a sort order. Repeat up to nine times in respect of fields below the first.

Finally, close the dialog.

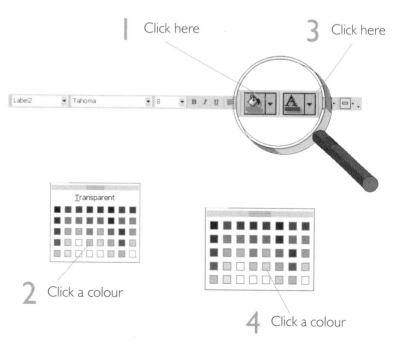

Specifying a border width

Access 2002 is supplied with a small number of pre-defined line widths which can be applied to controls. Note, however, that you can only apply the appropriate border to all four sides of a control: you can't specify which edges you border.

You must have opened the relevant report in Design View to carry out any of the procedures here.

With the relevant report open in Design View, click the control you want to amend. (If you want to amend more than one, hold down Shift at the same time.) Then do the following:

Click the arrow here

2 Click a border width

Specifying a border colour

With the relevant report open in Design View, click the control you want to amend. (If you want to amend more than one, hold down Shift at the same time.)

Then do the following:

Click the arrow here

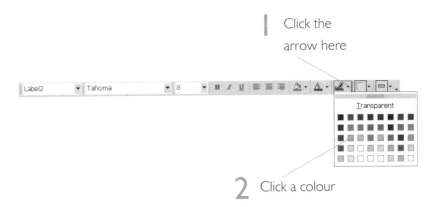

2 Click a colour

Applying special effects

Access 2002 lets you apply several special effects to controls. You can choose from:

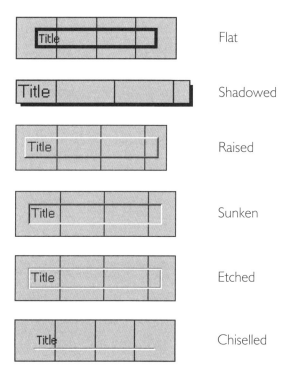

Flat

Shadowed

Raised

Sunken

Etched

Chiselled

With the relevant report open in Design View, click the control you want to amend. (If you want to select more than one, hold down Shift at the same time.) Then do the following:

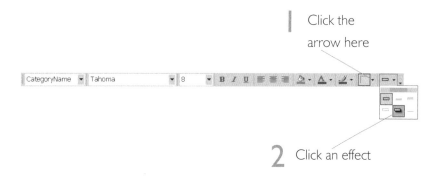

Click the arrow here

2 Click an effect

Previewing your report

You can't edit reports in Layout or Print Preview: you can only inspect them.

To leave Layout or Print Preview, press: Esc

To go to the next page in Print Preview, press Page Down. To go to the previous page, press Page Up.

To view two pages at once, click this button in the Print Preview toolbar:

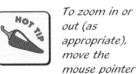

You can view reports in a special window which shows you how they'll look when printed. You can do this in two ways:

LayoutPreview — Access displays just enough data to give an accurate idea of what the report will look like

Print Preview — Access displays all the underlying table/query data, a screenful at a time

Previewing a report

Within Design view, pull down the View menu and do the following:

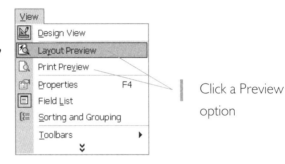

Click a Preview option

A report viewed in Print Preview:

To zoom in or out (as appropriate), move the mouse pointer (a magnifying glass) to the relevant area and left-click.

Saving your report

You can save reports in a special format (suffix: .SNP) which other users who don't have Access can read.

On the left of the Database window, click Reports, then select a report. Pull down the File menu and click Export. In the Save as type: field in the Export... dialog, select Snapshot Format (.snp). Choose a drive/folder combination in the usual way then name the snapshot and click Save. Access now launches the Snapshot Viewer with the report snapshot pre-loaded.*

Manually generated reports need to be saved to disk for later use.

Saving a report

Within Design view, pull down the File menu and do the following:

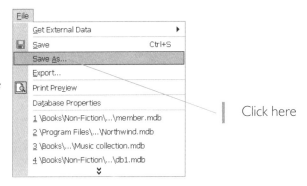

Click here

To view report snapshots in the Snapshot Viewer, click the Windows Start button. Then click Programs, Microsoft Office Tools, Microsoft Access Snapshot Viewer. In the Viewer, press Ctrl+O. Use the Open dialog to locate/ open the relevant .SNP file.

2 Name the report

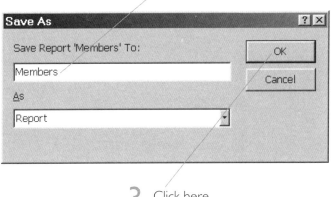

3 Click here

You can also view .SNP files in Internet Explorer 3.0 or later. In 5.x, press Ctrl+O. In the Open dialog, click Browse. In the further dialog, select All Files in the Files of type: box. Double-click a snapshot file and complete the dialogs.

Opening reports

When you open a report you've previously saved to disk, Access 2002 displays it in Preview mode. (Note also that when you create a new report with the Report Wizard or with AutoReport, by default Access previews it automatically – see earlier topics for more information on this.)

Opening a report

First, ensure the Database window is visible. Now do the following:

| Ensure the Reports tab is activated

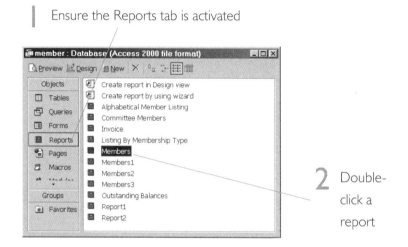

2 Double-click a report

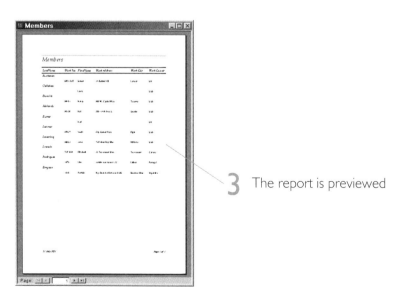

3 The report is previewed

Data access pages

In this chapter, you'll create specialised web files called data access pages. You'll use AutoPage to create them more conveniently and a wizard for when you need more complexity. You'll also create data access pages from scratch, on a stand-alone basis (to more faithfully retain the layout and formatting of other components) and from existing web pages. Then you'll open them within Access 2002 (including converting Access 2000 pages), customise them in Design view (including applying background themes and controls) and add/delete data in Page view.

Finally, you'll view your data access pages within Internet Explorer 5 (or higher) and save them to disk.

Covers

Chapter Nine

Data access pages – an overview

Data access pages are HTML files which are stored outside Access 2002 (although they appear in the Pages section of the Database window).

There are minor but telling differences between the way Internet Explorer versions 5 and 5.5 support data access pages (for example, in version 5 you can't select multiple controls in Design view.)

You must have Internet Explorer 5 or later to create or open data access pages.

This data access page has had no background theme applied.
To impose a theme from within Design View (see pages 159–160 for more on this view), pull down the Format menu and click Theme. In the Choose a Theme box in the Theme dialog, select a theme. Finally, click OK.

Data access pages are special web pages which let you view and work with Internet- or intranet-based Access 2002 databases. Data access pages (in the way you use them) resemble forms or reports and can also contain data from other programs (e.g. Excel 2002).

You can use data access pages to:

* analyse data

* enter and amend data

* review data

When users view a data access page in Internet Explorer 5.x, they see their own copy of the underlying data. The result is that:

* any presentational changes they make (data sorts etc.) are restricted to their copy

* changes to data are, however, reflected in the underlying database

You can also work with data access pages from within Access 2002 itself.

You can create data access pages:

* with the help of AutoPage

* with the help of a wizard

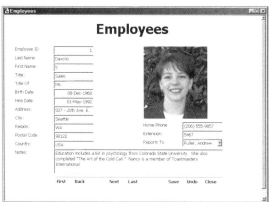

A data access page

Creating data access pages with AutoPage

To create stand-alone data access pages, close any open database. If the Task Pane isn't on-screen, choose View, Toolbars, Task Pane. In the Pane, click Blank Data Access Page. Use the dialog to locate/select a data source and click Open.

To save your completed data access page to disk, pull down the File menu and click Save As. Complete the Save As dialog, then click OK.

You can also save tables, forms, queries (Select or Crosstab) or reports as data access pages (this is a shortcut which produces data access pages which are closer to the original component).
In the Database window, select the relevant tab under Objects. On the right, select a database component. Pull down the File menu and click Save As. In the As field in the Save As dialog, select Data Access Page. Name the page and click OK. In the New Data Access Page dialog, choose where to save the page then click OK.

This method takes a specific record source and generates a data access page which utilises all the relevant fields.

1 In the Database window, ensure the Pages tab is activated

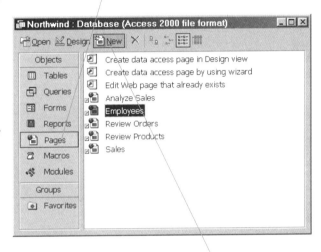

2 Click New

3 Click AutoPage: Columnar

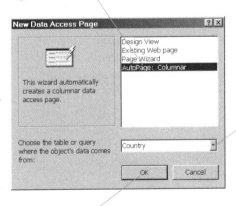

4 Click here; select the host table or query

5 Click here to create the new data access page

Creating data access pages with a wizard

This method produces a much more customised data access page.

You can also create data access pages by converting existing web pages.

Follow steps 1–3 on page 157. In 3, however, double-click Existing Web page instead. Use the dialog which launches to locate the relevant file, then click Open.

(The new page opens in Design View – customise it as necessary.)

To save your completed data access page to disk, pull down the File menu and click Save As. Complete the Save As dialog, then click OK.

After step 7, the final dialog launches. Name the data access page, choose to open or modify the completed page and click Finish.

Carry out steps 1–3 and 5 on page 157 (in 3, however, select Page Wizard)

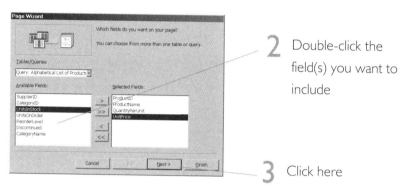

2 Double-click the field(s) you want to include

3 Click here

4 Optional – double-click a heading field

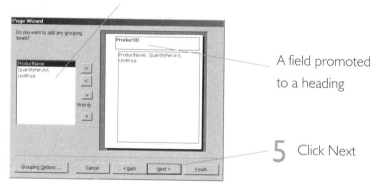

A field promoted to a heading

5 Click Next

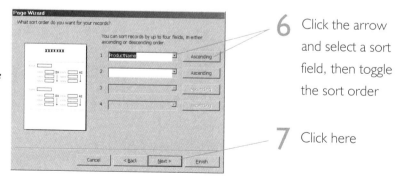

6 Click the arrow and select a sort field, then toggle the sort order

7 Click here

Creating data access pages manually

Sections are groups of related fields, all from the same table or query.

To switch between Design and Page views, pull down the View menu and click the relevant entry.

You can use Page view to add or delete data. Click the appropriate icon in the Record Navigation toolbar under the page body e.g.:

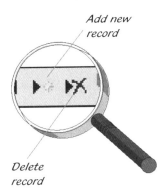

Add new record

Delete record

(Use standard techniques to edit, sort or filter data in Page view.)

To view a data access page in Internet Explorer 5 or higher, pull down the File menu and click Web Page Preview.

Carry out steps 1–3 and 5 on page 157 (in 3, however, select Design View)

Adding sections in Design view

Drag a section into the page

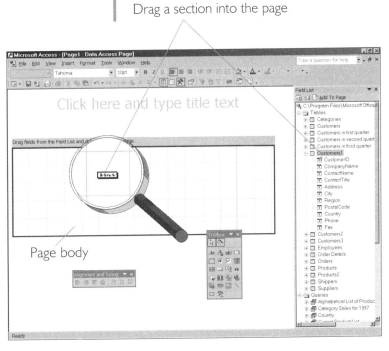

Page body

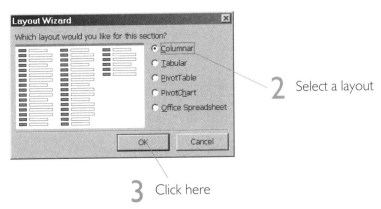

2 Select a layout

3 Click here

Adding fields in Design view

Follow step 1 on page 159

You can amend data access pages in Design view in a very similar way to forms and reports in Design View. For example, you can:

- *insert image-based hyperlinks or various controls via the Toolbox*
- *customise control fonts etc. with the Formatting (Page) toolbar*

However, to align controls in data access pages, use the dedicated Alignment and Sizing toolbar instead:

Data access pages created in Access 2000 are automatically converted for use in Access 2002 when you open them in Design view (Access 2002 creates a backup copy of the original).

To open a data access page, press F11. On the left of the Database window, select Pages. On the right, double-click a page.

3 Drag a field into the page

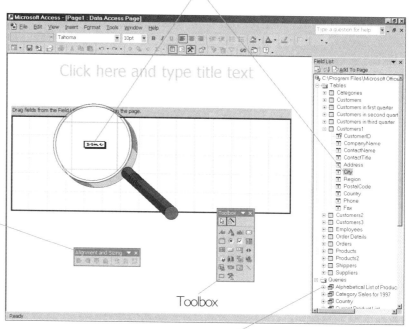

Toolbox

2 In the Task Pane, click ⊞ next to a section to reveal individual fields

4 The field is inserted – format this in line with pages 148–151

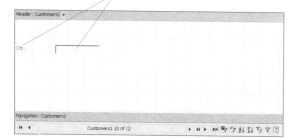

Creating graphs

In this chapter, you'll view your data graphically as a chart (so you can analyse it more effectively). You'll learn to create charts either as separate forms or reports in their own right or as part of existing forms/reports. You'll also create web charts in data access pages and link charts to specific records in the underlying table or query.

You'll go on to specify the chart type (either during the process of creation or subsequently) and edit charts in the underlying data source and in the base query. You'll also discover how to launch Microsoft Graph to reformat your charts in a variety of ways.

Finally, you'll save your completed chart to disk.

Covers

Chapter Ten

Graphs – an overview

Graphs give your data visual impact, and make it easier to understand. They also:

Use PivotCharts to display chart data dynamically and interactively.

- reveal hidden relationships between data

- make trends much more apparent

In one sense, graphs are similar to forms and reports: they let you view your data in a highly specific – and useful – fashion.

Graph creation

You create graphs in Access 2002 with the help of the Graph Wizard. You can use this wizard in two ways:

1. when you create a special form or report from scratch

2. from within existing forms or reports, in Design View

The first method is the easiest and quickest way to create a new graph. When you create a graph in this way, Access builds a new form or report with a single graph in it.

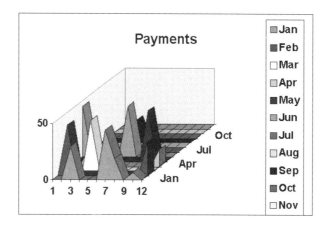

A new graph, excerpted from a form

When you use the second method, however, the result is almost identical. Both graphs can be extensively customised.

Creating a graph from scratch

First, ensure the Database window is visible. Then carry out the following steps:

Re step 1 – if you want to create your chart in a new form, select Forms instead.

1 To create a chart in a new report, select Reports

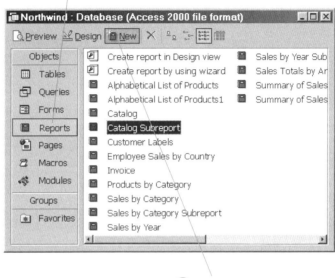

2 Click New

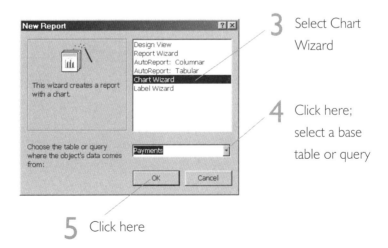

3 Select Chart Wizard

4 Click here; select a base table or query

5 Click here

Now carry out the following steps:

6 Double-click the fields
  you want to include

*At least one of
the fields you
select must
contain
numerical data
(e.g. – as here – currency
information).*

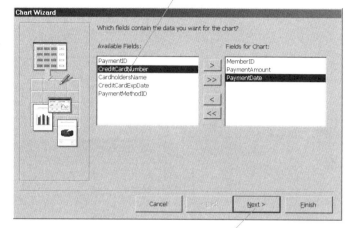

*Access 2002
provides a
potted
description of
each chart type
here:*

7 Click Next

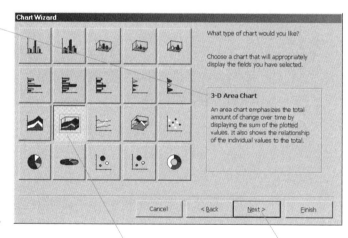

*Note that the
Chart Wizard
won't apply
some chart
types e.g.:*

• *Radar*

• *Surface*

*However, you can use the
techniques in the table on
page 174 to assign them to
completed charts.*

8 Click a chart format

9 Click Next

For a more comprehensive preview, see below.

In the next dialog, Access displays the selected fields as buttons. It makes assumptions which axes the fields should occupy, and displays a brief approximation of the result on the left of the dialog. If you want to change these assumptions, carry out steps 10–11 below, then follow step 12. If you don't, simply follow step 12:

10 Click and hold on a field button . . .

Perform steps 10–11 until the chart axes are represented by the correct

fields.

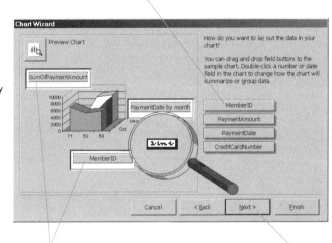

Re step 11 – when you drag the field button, the cursor changes. (See the magnified section in the dialog.)

11 Drag it to an axis box

12 Click Next

Previewing your chart...

13 If you want a rather more detailed preview of what your chart will look like, select the Preview Chart button in the top lefthand corner of the above dialog. Press Esc when you've finished with the Preview window

14 If the chart isn't what you want, click Back as often as required, then input the appropriate new chart parameters

15 Whether or not you followed step 13 and/or 14, carry out the additional steps overleaf

Carry out the final steps below:

|6 Name the chart

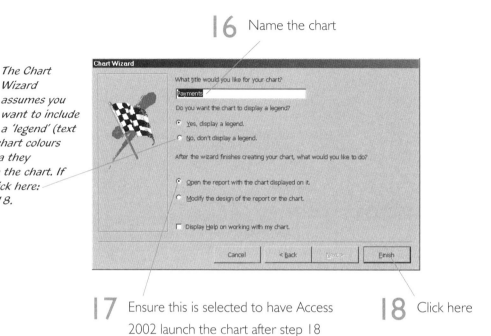

The Chart Wizard assumes you want to include a 'legend' (text which links chart colours with the data they represent) in the chart. If you don't, click here: before step 18.

|7 Ensure this is selected to have Access 2002 launch the chart after step 18

|8 Click here

This is the final result (in this instance, Access 2002 has opened the report which contains the new chart):

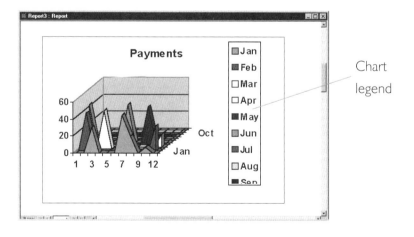

Chart legend

Creating an in-line graph

You can also run the Graph Wizard from within an existing form or report; however, the launch procedure is different.

First, open the relevant form or report (for how to do this, see Chapters 4 and 8 respectively). Then pull down the View menu and click Design View. Finally, pull down the Insert menu and do the following:

The example discussed in this and subsequent topics shows the addition of a graph to an existing form; the procedure is essentially the same for a report...

Click Chart

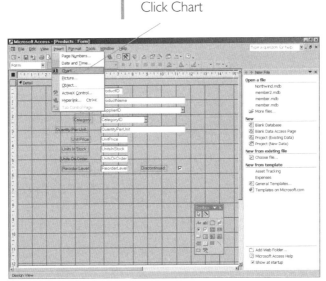

You can create web charts on data access pages. Open a data access page in Design view then pull down the Insert menu and select Office Chart. In the Toolbox, select this icon:

Drag out a chart on the data access page. Click the chart control once or twice (as required) then complete the Commands and Options dialog. For example, to base the chart on a table or query, select Data from a database table or query then click the Connection button. After the dialog changes, complete the fields in the Data Details and Type tabs.
Press Alt+F4 when you've finished.

The mouse pointer changes:

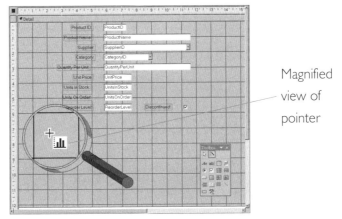

Magnified view of pointer

2 Position the transformed cursor at the point where you want the chart to begin then drag out the chart area

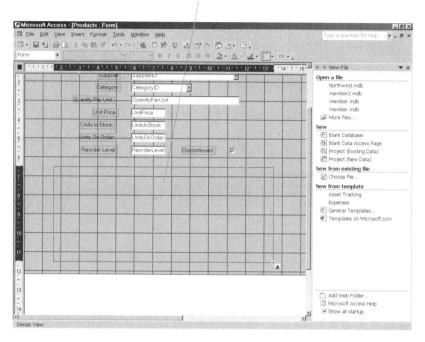

4 Click a table or query

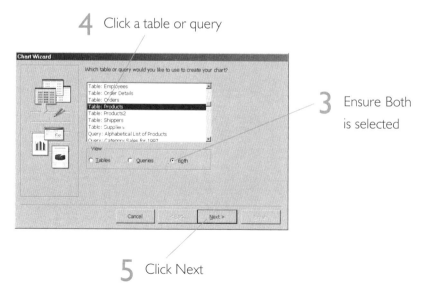

3 Ensure Both is selected

5 Click Next

6 Double-click the field(s) you want to include

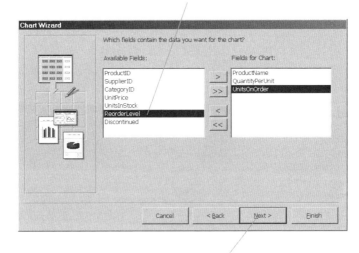

7 Click Next

8 Select a chart format

Access provides a potted description of the selected format here:

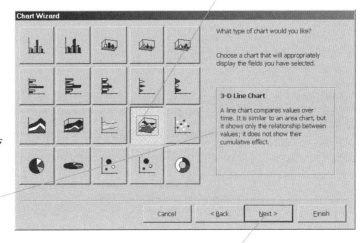

9 Click Next

Now, Access 2002 displays the selected fields as buttons and makes certain assumptions about which axes the fields should occupy. If you want to change these assumptions, carry out steps 10–11 below, then follow step 12. If you don't, simply follow step 12:

10 Click and hold on a field button . . .

Perform steps 10–11 until the chart axes are represented by the correct fields.

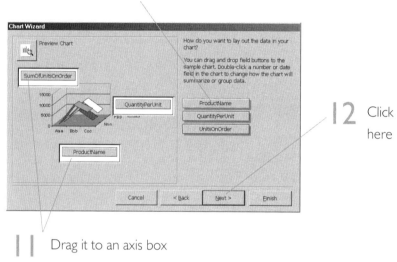

12 Click here

11 Drag it to an axis box

If you want to link the data in your graph with fields in the underlying form or report, do the following:

If you don't want to link any fields, simply carry out step 15.

13 Click here; select a field in the list

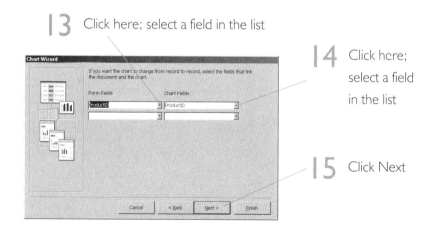

14 Click here; select a field in the list

15 Click Next

...cont'd

Carry out the final steps below:

16 Name the chart

The Chart Wizard assumes you want to include a 'legend' (text which links chart colours with the data they represent) in the chart. If you don't, click here: before step 17.

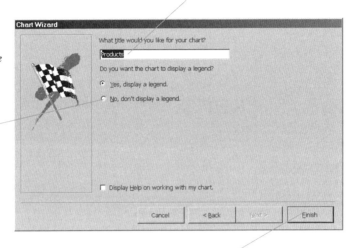

17 Click here

18 Here, Access 2002 has inserted the new chart into the original form:

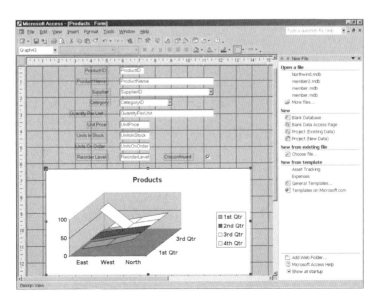

Amending graphs

However you use the Graph Wizard (either in the creation of a new form/report or from within an existing form/report), what actually happens is that Access launches a separate program – Microsoft Graph – behind the scenes. With the use of a kind of sleight of hand, Graph creates the chart and inserts it seamlessly into your form or report.

To modify existing charts, however, you have to make Microsoft Graph visible.

Launching Microsoft Graph

This is a two-stage process. The first stage is to launch (in Design View) the form or report which contains the chart you want to alter.

Make sure the Database window is visible. Then do the following:

If you're short of hard disk space, you can convert charts (but not record-linked charts – see the HOT TIP below) into pictures. However, charts which have been converted can no longer be edited.
   Select the chart in Design view. Pull down the Format menu and click Change To, Image.

Re step 1 – if you want to edit a form-based chart instead, select Forms.

You can bind a chart to a specific record in the underlying table or query, so that it only reflects data from that record.
   In Design view, right-click the chart and select Properties. In the dialog, select the Data tab. In the LinkChildFields and LinkMasterFields boxes, type in a field name (but note that it must be a name you can see by clicking in the Row Source box).

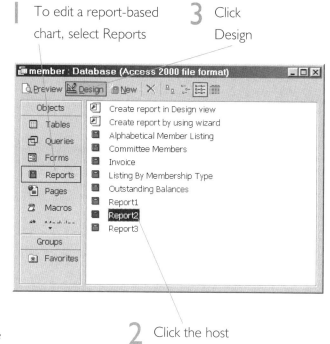

1 To edit a report-based chart, select Reports

3 Click Design

2 Click the host form or report

In the second stage, do the following:

You can preview charts in Graph. To do this, pull down the View menu and click Print Preview.

(To return to your chart in Design View, press Esc.)

To resize a chart, click it in Design view. Drag one of the resizing handles in or out.

(To move the chart, click it – the pointer changes to a hand. Drag the chart to a new location.)

You can only display a limited number of toolbars in Microsoft Graph (not, for instance, the Task Pane).

For how to use the Datasheet and Chart windows, see page 174.

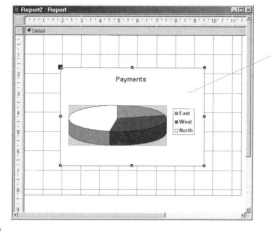

4 Double-click anywhere in the chart area

5 In Graph, the Datasheet window launches

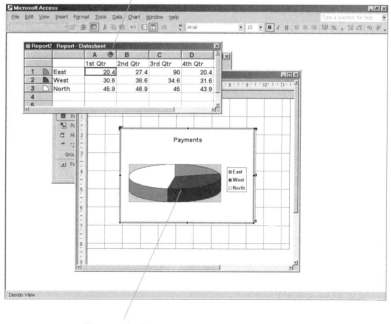

Chart window

The changes described in pages 172–174 are formatting-based. *However, you can also amend the data on which a chart is structured. You can simply edit the table which underpins the chart within the table itself, or you can amend the chart query (when you create a chart with the Chart Wizard, Access generates a specific query based on the choices made).*

To edit the chart query, right-click the chart in Design view and choose Properties. In the dialog, ensure the Data tab is active. Click in the Row Source field and select:

to the right. The Query Builder launches. Use this to amend the query e.g. add extra fields. Close the various dialogs.

To save your finished graph to disk, follow the relevant Save procedures discussed in Chapters 4 (Forms) and 8 (Reports).

Microsoft Graph consists of two components (click either component to activate it):

- the Datasheet window

- the Chart window

You can use the Datasheet window to enter/amend data; it works as a mini-table (see Chapter 3 for how to use it).

Using the Chart window

Carry out any of the procedures in the following table:

To amend the chart type	Pull down the Chart menu and click Chart Type. Activate the Standard Types tab in the Chart Type dialog. Select a new type/sub-type combination and click OK to apply it
To apply a custom format	Pull down the Chart menu and click Chart Type. Activate the Custom Types tab in the dialog. Select a chart type. Click OK to apply it
To change the font and/or type size for legends	Select the text by clicking it. Pull down the Format menu and click Font. In the dialog, click a new typeface in the Font: field. Or select a new type size in the Size: box. Click OK to apply your changes

When you've finished working in Graph, click anywhere outside the chart. You're returned to Access 2002, and the original chart is automatically updated.

Printing your data

In this chapter, you'll print out your data. Before you do this, however, you'll learn how to ensure that the overall page layout is correct. You'll revise margin settings (including globally); allocate a page size/orientation; specify column dimensions (for forms and reports); and – in the case of data access pages – specify which frames print.

You'll go on to preview your work, using the Access 2002 Print Preview window, before printing out a map of database relationships; ensuring your print-out shows subdatasheets (if required); customising print settings; and printing your data. Finally, you'll also print directly from component shortcuts and print more quickly (via a method which bypasses the Print dialog).

Covers

Chapter Eleven

Printing – an overview

Access 2002 handles printing in broadly the same way, irrespective of whether you're printing tables, forms, reports, queries or data access pages.

Data access pages have additional options – see page 184.

In spite of this, however, there are differences:

- tables and queries have fewer incidental settings you can specify before you begin a print-run (the available settings are limited to margins and page size/orientation)

- with forms and reports, you can specify a variety of additional layout and page setup settings (principally relating to multi-column documents) before you begin printing

In spite of these discrepancies, you can always preview your work before you commit yourself to printing it. This is advisable as:

Reports can be viewed in Layout (as well as Print) Preview – see page 152 for more detailed information on both.

- the Access Print Preview screen provides a fully WYSIWYG (What You See Is What You Get) representation of what your data will look like when printed

- Access data (especially in tables) frequently spreads across more than one page; Print Preview gives you a bird's-eye view of this process in operation

A form in Print Preview:

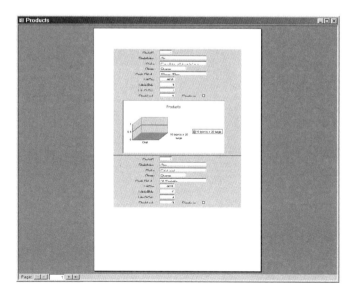

Page Setup issues

Page setup settings are stored with forms and reports, so you only have to enter them once for each component. With a table, data access page or query, however, you have to input them each time you want to print it.

You can also specify page setup settings for data access pages.

In step 1, select Pages. In step 2, double-click a page. Follow step 3. The Page Setup dialog differs slightly from the version overleaf – do the following:

* *click in the Size field and select a page size*
* *in the Header and Footer fields, type in text you want to appear on every page*
* *select an orientation*
* *enter margin settings*

Click OK when you've finished.

To set default margins, choose Tools, Options. Select the General tab and input settings in the Print margins section. Click OK.

If you intend to print tables, queries, forms or reports, you need to ensure that the correct page setup/layout settings are in force before you do so.

With the Database window open, do the following:

1 Activate the Tables, Queries, Forms or Reports tabs, as appropriate

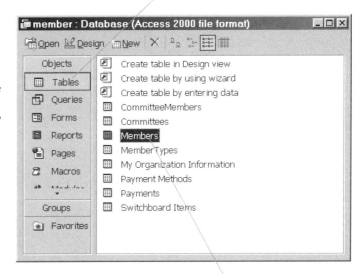

2 Double-click a table, query, form or report

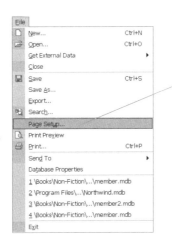

3 Pull down the File menu and click Page Setup

Setting margin sizes

Follow steps 1–3 on page 177 then do the following:

In forms, this field is Print Data Only. Select this to ignore gridlines, labels and borders when printing:

In tables, ensure this is selected to print column headings.

4 Ensure the Margins tab is active

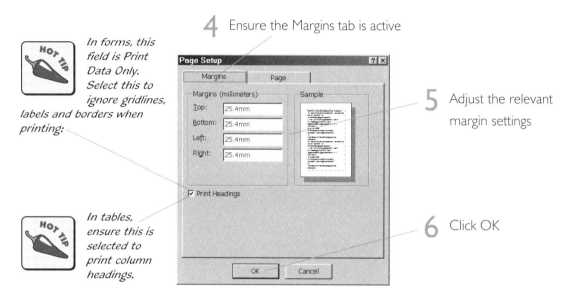

5 Adjust the relevant margin settings

6 Click OK

Setting page size/orientation

Follow steps 1–3 on page 177. Carry out step 4 below, then 5 and/or 6, as appropriate. Finally, follow step 7:

Re step 5 – note that the following types of orientation are available:

Portrait

Landscape

4 Ensure the Page tab is active

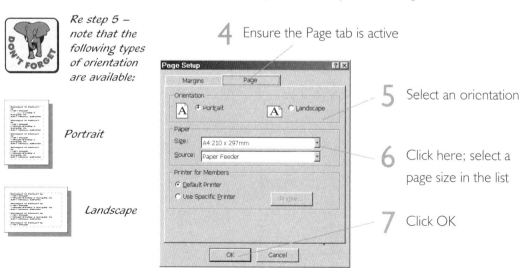

5 Select an orientation

6 Click here; select a page size in the list

7 Click OK

Specifying column layouts

In forms or reports, you can determine:

- how many columns data prints in

- the inter-column spacing

- the column width and/or height

- the gap between rows

- the order in which Access 2002 prints fields within records

Follow steps 1–3 on page 177 then carry out step 4 below. Follow steps 5–8, as appropriate, then step 9:

Note that this version of the Page Setup dialog only launches over forms and reports.

(For how to use the table- and query-specific version, see page 178.)

5 Type in the no. of columns

4 Activate the Columns tab

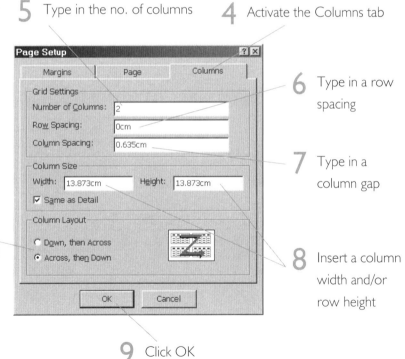

6 Type in a row spacing

7 Type in a column gap

8 Insert a column width and/or row height

Click the appropriate option here: to specify print direction:

Down, then Across

Across, then Down

Finally, follow step 9.

9 Click OK

Launching Print Preview

You can preview any database component before printing it.

First, launch the Database window. Then carry out the following steps:

When you open a report, Access automatically launches it in Preview mode.

| Activate the Tables, Queries, Forms or Reports tabs, as appropriate

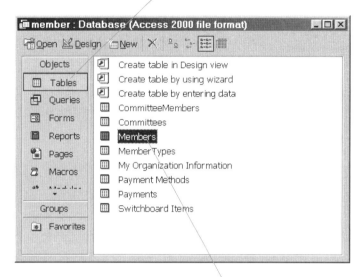

To preview database components after you've opened them, just follow step 3

(See page 152 for more detailed information on how to preview reports.)

2 Double-click a table, query, form or report

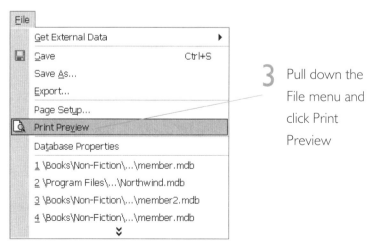

3 Pull down the File menu and click Print Preview

Using Print Preview

When you opt to preview a database component, Access 2002 launches a special Print Preview window showing how the component will look when printed:

Print Preview toolbar

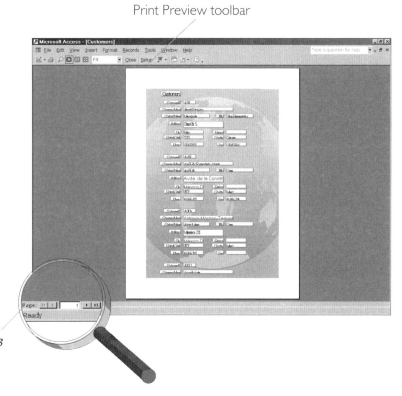

This is the Print Preview Record Gauge: (See page 103 for how to use it.)

The Print Preview window has its own dedicated toolbar (see above). You can use this to:

- zoom in or out (there are two methods)

- apply a preset Zoom percentage (e.g. 150%, 200%)

- specify the view spread (1 or 2 pages)

- initiate printing immediately

You can also use the Record Gauge in the bottom lefthand corner of the Print Preview window to (among other things) move to a precise page instantly.

You can start printing immediately from Print Preview. Click this button:

Zooming in and out – method 1

Refer to the Print Preview toolbar and do the following:

Click here

to alternate between:

- Full Page view (where the whole page is visible in the Print Preview window); and

- whichever Zoom level was previously set (see page 183)

Zooming in and out – method 2

You can also use a variation on the above technique to select which area of the database component you want to zoom in or out on.

Carry out the above procedure, then position the mouse pointer over the section of the Print Preview window you want to view – the pointer becomes a magnifying glass:

Left-click to zoom in or out

To specify your own Zoom %, omit steps 1–2. Instead, type in a % here: then press Enter.

Applying a preset Zoom percentage

Refer to the Print Preview toolbar and do the following:

Click here

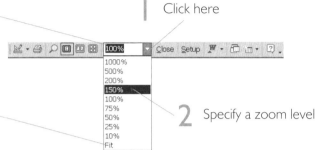

Re step 2 – click Fit to have Access 2002 choose a Zoom level which displays your table, query, form or report optimally, according to the size of the window.

2 Specify a zoom level

Specifying the view spread

Refer to the Print Preview toolbar and do the following:

Click here to view a single page

Click here to view two pages

To display more than one or two pages, click this button instead:

Now do the following:

Select a preview configuration

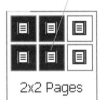

2x2 Pages

A one-page spread

A two-page spread

Printing your data

You can print a diagram showing database relationships.

Pull down the Tools menu and click Relationships. The Relationships window launches. Pull down the File menu and click Print Relationships. Access generates a report containing the necessary diagram. Print it in the usual way.

You can also print data access pages. In step 1, select Pages. In step 2, double-click a page. Follow step 3. Complete the Print dialog – this is basically the same as for any other component except that you can also specify which frames print.

If you're printing a datasheet which contains one or more subdatasheets which you also want to print, first click the [+] next to them to expand them.

If you opened a datasheet in step 2 and only want to print specific records, select them before you follow step 3.

Stage 1 – preparing to print

First, preview the database component you want to print (for how to do this, see pages 180–183). Close the Print Preview window and launch the Database window. Then do the following:

1 Activate the Tables, Queries, Forms or Reports tabs, as appropriate

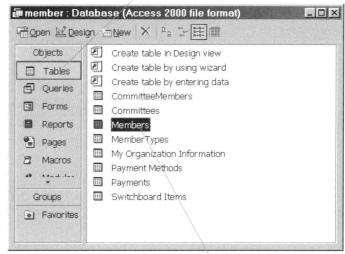

2 Double-click a table, query, form or report

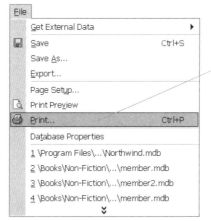

3 Pull down the File menu and click Print

If you print from within a form which is open in Design view, it prints in Form view.

If you've created a desktop shortcut for a database component, you can print the component from the shortcut. Right-click the shortcut icon and choose Print in the menu.

Stage 2 – specifying the print settings

You can:

• specify the printer you want to use

• print the whole database component (the default)

• print a specific page range (e.g. pages 10–15)

• confine the print run to records you selected earlier

• specify the number of copies printed

• turn collation off or on. Collation is the process whereby Access 2002 prints one full copy at a time. For instance, if you're printing 5 copies of a 12-page database, when collation is active Access 2002 prints pages 1–12 of the first copy, 1–12 of the second copy, and so on…

Carry out any of steps 1–5 below. Finally, follow step 6:

If you need to adjust your printer settings, click here:
before carrying out step 6.
   (See your printer's manual for how to complete the resulting dialogs.)

Click here; select a printer in the list

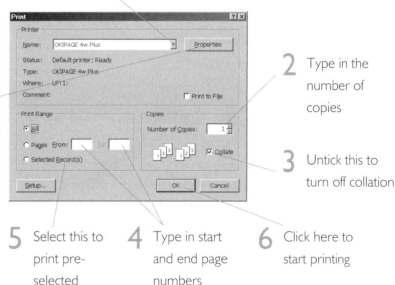

2 Type in the number of copies

3 Untick this to turn off collation

5 Select this to print pre-selected records only

4 Type in start and end page numbers

6 Click here to start printing

Printing – the fast-track approach

There are occasions when you'll merely want to print out your work:

- without having to invoke the Print dialog

- with the current settings applying

- with a single mouse click

One reason for doing this is proofing. Irrespective of how thoroughly you check documents on-screen, there will always be errors and deficiencies which, with the best will in the world, are difficult or impossible to pick up. By initiating printing with the minimum of delay, you can check your work that much more rapidly...

For this reason, Access 2002 provides a printing method which is especially quick and easy to use.

Printing with the current print options

First, ensure your printer is ready and on-line. Refer to the appropriate toolbar and do the following:

This example shows the Table Datasheet toolbar but many toolbars have a Print icon.

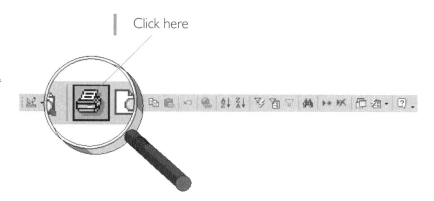

Click here

2 The active database component starts to print immediately, using the current defaults

Index